D1162442

To

KNOW
HIM *by*
NAME

ידוה

Y A H W E H

RABBI KIRT A.
SCHNEIDER

CHARISMA
HOUSE

To Know Him by Name by Rabbi Kirt A. Schneider
Published by Charisma House, an imprint of Charisma Media
600 Rinehart Road, Lake Mary, Florida 32746

Copyright © 2023 by Rabbi Kirt A. Schneider. All rights reserved

Unless otherwise noted, all Scripture quotations are taken from the (NASB®) New American Standard Bible®, Copyright © 1960, 1971, 1977, 1995 by The Lockman Foundation. Used by permission. All rights reserved. www.lockman.org

Scripture quotations marked AMP are from the Amplified® Bible (AMP), Copyright © 2015 by The Lockman Foundation. Used by permission. www.Lockman.org

Scripture quotations marked KJV are from the King James Version of the Bible.

Scripture quotations marked MEV are from the Modern English Version. Copyright © 2014 by Military Bible Association. Used by permission. All rights reserved.

Scripture quotations marked NIV are taken from the Holy Bible, New International Version®, NIV®. Copyright © 1973, 1978, 1984, 2011 by Biblica, Inc.® Used by permission of Zondervan. All rights reserved worldwide. www.zondervan.com. The "NIV" and "New International Version" are trademarks registered in the United States Patent and Trademark Office by Biblica, Inc.®

Scripture quotations marked NKJV are taken from the New King James Version®. Copyright © 1982 by Thomas Nelson. Used by permission. All rights reserved.

All italicized words and phrases in Scripture quotations are added by the author for emphasis.

While the author has made every effort to provide accurate internet addresses at the time of publication, neither the publisher nor the author assumes any responsibility for errors or for changes that occur after publication. Further, the publisher does not have any control over and does not assume any responsibility for author or third-party websites or their content.

For more Spirit-led resources, visit charismahouse.com and the author's website at discoveringthejewishjesus.com.

Cataloging-in-Publication Data is on file with the Library of Congress.
International Standard Book Number: 978-1-63641-220-7
E-book ISBN: 978-1-63641-221-4

23 24 25 26 27 — 9 8 7 6 5 4 3 2 1
Printed in the United States of America

Most Charisma Media products are available at special quantity discounts for bulk purchase for sales promotions, premiums, fund-raising, and educational needs. For details, call us at (407) 333-0600 or visit our website at www.charismamedia.com.

CONTENTS

Part III: The Hebrew Names of Messiah

Part IV: Our Response to Who God Is

INTRODUCTION

KNOWING THE NAMES and titles of God as revealed in the Hebrew Bible, or the Old Testament, is much more than an intellectual exercise. By understanding them, we don't just learn interesting information; we discover who God truly is and who He desires to be for us.

In our modern culture, names identify a person, place, or thing. However, in the ancient Hebrew culture a name had symbolic and often prophetic significance. When God revealed His names and titles to the world through the Hebrew people, He was showing us a dimension of who He is—His character, His purposes, and His will.

By coming to know God's names and titles, you will actually come to better know Him. We cannot see God with our physical eyes, but we can know Him through His self-revelation.

Perhaps you remember back during your high school years when you met someone you found attractive. If you really wanted to get to know the person, what was the first thing you did? You tried to find out their name because knowing their name was the first step in building a relationship with them.

So it is with God. I am convinced that when we know God's names and titles and we begin declaring them, trusting in them, depending upon them, and taking hold of Him through them, we will be brought into greater faith and intimacy with Him, and ultimately we will have greater victory in our lives.

When God reveals Himself to us through His names and titles, He doesn't do it just so we will know them; He does it so we can lay hold of and respond to them. For example, when the Lord revealed Himself as Yahweh Yireh, which means "the Lord our Provider" or "the Lord will provide," it was so we would respond to that name in faith, saying, "Lord, I trust that You will provide for me."

Again, we learn God's names and titles not as just an intellectual exercise. God's purpose in revealing Himself is to challenge our faith so that every time we claim one of His names or titles, we will take hold of it and move out in faith toward Him.

Many of us have a wrong concept of God because Satan has blinded us to the truth of who He truly is. We have been deceived into believing that our Father is a harsh God of wrath and judgment. We tend to see Him as being mostly mad instead of mostly glad. An example of this is found in the parable of the talents in Matthew 25:14–30. In this parable, a man representing Yeshua (Jesus) was going on a journey, and he entrusted his possessions to his three servants.

To the first servant the master gave ten talents, to the second he gave five talents, and to the third he gave just one talent. When the man returned from his journey, the first and second servants had each doubled the number of talents they had been given. When the master approached the third servant, the man responded by saying, "Master, I knew you to be a hard man....And I was afraid, and went away and hid your talent in the ground. See, you have what is yours" (Matt. 25:24–25).

This servant was ultimately cast aside and his talent taken away because he had a misconception of his master. He wrongly understood his master to be harsh, and it affected the way he thought and the decisions he made and caused him to be unwilling to take a risk with the talent he was given. Like that servant, we too can make wrong decisions in life when we have a wrong concept of God. When we see Him as harsh instead of as the loving person He truly is, we aren't willing to trust Him with our lives and all we have been given.

Actually, one of the greatest forms of idol worship and a major offense to God is to have a wrong concept of Him and thus relate to Him inappropriately. We must step out from Satan's lies and see the Lord for who He really is, a loving God who desires a relationship and unity with us.

Hear this: the very essence of God's nature and character is revealed to us through His Hebrew names and titles. It is that way with biblical names in general. We see an example of this with the name Ya`akov (Jacob), which actually means "heel grabber" or "one who cheats."[1] When Rebekah was giving birth to the twins Jacob and Esau, Jacob grabbed Esau's heel as they were coming out of the womb, as if he was trying to keep Esau from coming out first. (Even though Esau was born first, Jacob later stole his brother's birthright.)

Another example of a name revealing a person's nature and character is Jesus' Hebrew name, Yeshua. It means salvation, and through Yeshua mankind receives salvation. Scripture says, "You shall call His name Jesus [Yeshua], for He will save His people from their sins" (Matt. 1:21).

One of the greatest examples of a name revealing the essence of a person is in Exodus 34. When Moshe (Moses) asked to see God's glory, the Lord responded by telling Moses that He wouldn't be able to show him the fullness of His glory, but He would allow Moses to discover Him as He proclaimed His name.

When Father God declared His name to Moses, He filled Moses with revelation knowledge of who He was because, once again, a name reveals the essence of a person:

> Then the LORD passed by in front of him and proclaimed, "The LORD, the LORD God, compassionate and gracious, slow to anger, and abounding in lovingkindness and truth; who keeps lovingkindness for thousands, who forgives iniquity, transgression and sin; yet He will by no means leave the guilty unpunished, visiting the iniquity of fathers on the children and on the grandchildren to the third and fourth generations." Moses made haste to bow low toward the earth and worship.
>
> —Exodus 34:6–8

As you read these pages, I want you to consider who God is to you. Is He your provider, your peace, your Savior, your Shepherd, your victorious healer? When you take hold of the revelation God has given to you in His names and titles, it will strengthen your faith, give you peace, and bring victory to your life.

A Word About Terminology

Before we begin, I want to make a quick note about the terminology I use. For the purposes of this book, the terms *Israel, the Hebrews,* and *the Jewish people* are used interchangeably. Technically there is a difference. God's revelation first came to the Hebrews, those who had crossed over into the realm of walking with the one true God. From the Hebrews, God formed the people of Israel. Due to Israel's exile into the various parts of the world, ten of the twelve tribes are considered lost. Most Jewish people today are from the tribes of Judah, from which we get the word *Jew,* and Benjamin. But for the purposes of this book, when I use the terms *Jew* or *the Jewish people,* I'm using them more generally, the way Paul did in the Book of Romans to refer to all of Israel.

PART I

THE HEBREW TITLES OF GOD

CHAPTER 1

ELOHIM—
THE CREATOR

I N THE VERY first verse of the Old Testament, in the Book of Genesis, called Bereshit ("in the beginning") in Hebrew, God reveals Himself to mankind as Elohim:

> In the beginning God [Elohim] created the heavens and the earth.
>
> —GENESIS 1:1

The Hebrew word *Elohim* is a title, not a personal name. It comes from the singular word *El*, which is typically translated "God" but also means "strength," "might," or "power." The term was widely used in ancient times, including by pagan nations such as the Canaanites, who also referred to their false gods as El. Because of this, when El was used to refer to the one true God of Israel, additional words were almost always included that further described God's attributes, thus distinguishing Him from the false pagan gods. Two examples of this are El Shaddai (God Almighty) and El Elyon (God Most High), which we will examine in later chapters.

1

A Multidimensional God

It is also important to note that Elohim is a plural form of El. In Hebrew, when *-im* is added to the end of a word, the term becomes plural. For instance, there is a type of angelic being called a seraph and another called a cherub, but when *-im* is added, as in *seraphim* or *cherubim*, the terms are referring to more than one seraph or cherub.

The plurality of *Elohim* does not indicate that there is more than one God; rather, it speaks of the multidimensional nature of God, a concept that is difficult for many to fully understand. This multidimensional nature of Elohim, revealed throughout the Scriptures, demonstrates that God has relationship within Himself. We see the first example of this in the Book of Genesis.

> Then God said, "Let *Us* make man in *Our* image, according to *Our* likeness."…God created man in His own image, in the image of God He created him; male and female He created them.
>
> —Genesis 1:26–27

To whom was Elohim speaking when He used the words *Us* and *Our*? The rabbis teach that He was talking to the angels, but I believe that when God said, "Let Us make man in Our image, according to Our likeness," He was speaking to Himself, displaying that He has relationship within Himself.

Several other examples of this multidimensional nature of Elohim are found in the New Testament, called the B'rit Hadashah in Hebrew. In the Gospel of John, for instance, Jesus is referred to in the mystery of the Word.

> In the beginning was the Word, and the Word was with God, and the Word was God. He was in the beginning with God. All things came into being through Him, and apart from Him nothing came into being that has come into being.
>
> —JOHN 1:1–3

Jesus, the Word, was with God, and He is God. This relationship between the Son and the Father is a mystery that is difficult for us to comprehend. But in John 1:18 we read that Yeshua, "the only begotten God…is in the bosom of the Father." This denotes love, relationship, and community within the Godhead.

Consider also when Yeshua was baptized in the Jordan River. The Scriptures say: "After being baptized, Jesus came up immediately from the water; and behold, the heavens were opened, and he saw the Spirit of God descending as a dove and lighting on Him, and behold, a voice out of the heavens said, 'This is My beloved Son, in whom I am well-pleased'" (Matt. 3:16–17).

Notice that all three persons of the Godhead were present. The Son (Yeshua) was being immersed, the Father spoke from heaven, and the Holy Spirit (Ruach HaKodesh) descended as a dove upon the Son.

Messiah Yeshua also addressed the Father as He hung on the cross. Matthew 27:46 says, "About the ninth hour Jesus cried out with a loud voice, saying, 'Eli, Eli, lama sabachthani?' that is, 'My God, My God, why have You forsaken Me?'" *Eli* is a form of *Elohim*.

Elohim's multidimensional nature demonstrates that relationship exists within Him. I believe the concept of family units on earth—fathers, mothers, brothers, and sisters—is a manifestation of the fact that there is relationship within God. He is One, yet He is not lonely because He has relationship within Himself!

Recently the Lord revealed to me something I found mind-blowing and transformative as I was studying the Book of Genesis and read, "Let Us make man in our image" (1:26). As a teacher on the Hebrew roots of the Bible, I have taught for years that the "Us" reveals the communication between the Father and Son. But another level of revelation of this is that *God is Us*. Think about this. God is an "Us." God Himself is community. He is a God who is not alone. He is Us; there is relationship within Him. So when you and I come into relationship with Him, we come into relationship with the Us. This means we are always in community because God is community. This is why the New Testament stresses that we are the body of Messiah and we are all connected to one another.

Getting hold of this concept that God Himself is an Us will spur us to relate to others with an "us" mentality instead of a "me vs. them" mentality. So in all our relationships, we won't look at the person we're in relationship with only as a separate individual; instead, we will understand that together we are an "us," and we will look for what is good for both of us. We will see ourselves not as lone individuals functioning apart from others but as connected and looking for the common good of all the parties in the relationship.

Knowing that God is an Us helps me not to feel alone and, as Philippians 2:4 says, to look out not only for my own interests but also for the interests of others, because I realize it's not about me anymore; it's about us. God is an Us.

It is also worth noting that sometimes a Hebrew word is made plural for greater emphasis. In other words, when you say *Elohim*, you're actually saying God is the supreme and only true God. The *-im* adds extra emphasis on who God is.

The Creator of the Universe

God's Hebrew title Elohim reveals to us that He is the one true, all-powerful God who is the ruler and Creator of the universe! It truly is both mind-boggling and satanic that our schools are teaching children they were created through the process of macroevolution instead of teaching them the truth that Elohim Himself created them.

This false teaching of macroevolution has caused so many children to lose their sense of identity and purpose. As a result, they feel lost in life. If God did not create us, then we must find purpose, meaning, and identity somewhere else. This is why we have such an increase in immorality and addictions of all kinds. When our children understand the truth that they have been created in the image of Elohim, they will have a strong sense of identity and purpose and live healthy lives.

I want to draw your attention again to Genesis 1. Notice that in the beginning God created them male and female:

> God created man in His own image, in the image of God He created him; male and female He created them. God blessed them; and God said to them, "Be fruitful and multiply."
>
> —Genesis 1:27–28

As is obvious to all, men cannot multiply through sexual relationships with other men nor can women multiply through sexual relationships with other women. This should make it clear to everyone who is open to the truth that the current trend of gender fluidity, homosexuality, and transgenderism is not in alignment with the divine design of creation.

When we understand that we were created by Elohim in His very image—that His very DNA is in us—we will walk in a state of conscious blessing. He personally and specifically breathed you into existence for a purpose. Knowing this will change how you think of yourself. You'll begin declaring, "I'm created in the image of Elohim!" You'll start viewing yourself as more than just your occupation. Whether you're a doctor, lawyer, construction worker, secretary, teacher, or housewife, you'll understand that you've been created for greater things and that there is more to you than you realize.

When you truly know that Elohim created you, your focus will change from the temporal to the eternal and from the worldly to the heavenly. You will stop identifying yourself by what the world thinks or says about you—by how short, tall, fat, or thin you are; the color of your skin; your occupation; or how much money you have.

Only when you realize that you are Elohim's creation will you understand He's the only One who has the answer to who you are. He's the One who has the key to unlock your soul. Only Elohim can give you revelation about who you really are. Everyone in the world is searching for identity in life, and if you do not find your identity in Elohim, you will look for it in the things of this world: money, social status, beauty, knowledge, sports, career success, and the like. Of course, all these counterfeits will leave you completely empty because you were created by God for His purposes. Your identity can be found only in Elohim, your Creator.

The Bible says, "For from Him and through Him and to Him are all things" (Rom. 11:36). When you know God as Elohim, your life will surely change. He will heal your self-image so you can experience greater freedom in Him. He will reveal *good things* to you about yourself that you never knew, and you'll discover that you're much more than you ever thought. You'll discover how much Elohim loves you and how valuable and significant you are. God's Word says: "God created man in His own image, in the image of God He created him; male and female He created them....God saw all that He had made, and behold, it was *very good*" (Gen. 1:27, 31).

One of my favorite passages of Scripture is Psalm 139, where David gives thanks to his Creator for making him so fearfully and wonderfully:

> For You formed my inward parts; You wove me in my mother's womb. *I will give thanks to You, for I am fearfully and wonderfully made*; wonderful are Your works, and my soul knows it very well.
>
> —Psalm 139:13–14

Just like David, you too have been fearfully, incredibly, supernaturally, exquisitely, and wonderfully created by Elohim, the Creator.

CHAPTER 2

EL ELYON—GOD
MOST HIGH

As discussed in the previous chapter, *El* is a Hebrew word meaning "god" that was commonly used by many of the pagan nations during the time of the ancient Israelites. The Canaanites, for example, called their gods El. But it was the one true God—the God of Avraham (Abraham), Yitz'chak (Isaac), and Ya'akov (Jacob)—who proclaimed that He, the God of Israel, is not only El (God) but El Elyon (God Most High), the highest, exalted One.

As I have studied the Scriptures and the different facets of God's nature revealed through His names, I've found the Lord often makes Himself known as El Elyon when He wants to impress us with His sovereignty over the earth. We see this in Genesis 14, where God first revealed Himself as El Elyon.

Abraham, then called Abram, received word that four kings had conspired to attack Sodom and Gomorrah and had taken his nephew Lot hostage and seized all Lot's possessions. Abram gathered 318 trained men from his household and pursued the kings, not only rescuing Lot and reclaiming his goods but also saving the others who had been taken captive and recovering their possessions as well. It was a tremendous victory.

Afterward Abram met Melchizedek, a priest of El Elyon who blessed Abram in the name of God Most High.

> And Melchizedek king of Salem brought out bread and wine; now he was a priest of God Most High [El Elyon]. He blessed him and said, "Blessed be Abram of God Most High [El Elyon], possessor of heaven and earth; and blessed be God Most High [El Elyon], who has delivered your enemies into your hand."
> —Genesis 14:18–20

The New Testament teaches that as a king and priest, Melchizedek foreshadowed Messiah Jesus, who is the incarnation of El Elyon. The Scriptures say of Yeshua: "He became to all those who obey Him the source of eternal salvation, being designated by God as a high priest according to the order of Melchizedek" (Heb. 5:9–10).

When Abram and Melchizedek met, Abram received bread and wine from Melchizedek and then gave the priest-king a tenth of all he had. This is in stark contrast to the way Abram responded to the king of Sodom when he offered him some of the spoils of the war. Instead of accepting the king's gift, Abram said, "I have sworn to the LORD God Most High [El Elyon], possessor of heaven and earth, that I will not take a thread or a sandal thong or anything that is yours, for fear you would say, 'I have made Abram rich.' I will take nothing except what the young men have eaten, and the share of the men who went with me" (Gen. 14:22–24).

We see in this passage that when Abram came to know God as El Elyon, he vowed to serve Him alone. He knew no one—no god, enemy, or king—could hold a candle to the Most High God. I pray the same revelation grips your heart and mine. When we realize that our God is El Elyon, we'll no longer be fearful in the midst of our enemies. We'll have the courage to face them because we trust that El Elyon has given us authority over them and ultimately the victory will be ours. Yeshua told us in Matthew 28:18 that "all authority has been given to Me in heaven and on earth."

El Elyon not only has authority over all our enemies, but He has authority over all our circumstances. As we develop confidence in El Elyon, we will enjoy greater peace in life because we know in the end we will overcome no matter what obstacles we face.

El Elyon gave Abram the victory over his enemies not only to show Abram that He is sovereign over his foes but also to reveal Himself as sovereign over all things in the universe. Just as Abram was confident that El Elyon was sovereign in his life, we too can be confident that the "possessor of heaven and earth" is sovereign in our lives. Because we are born of Him and greater is He that is in us than He that is in the world, we can feel secure in God.

The King of All Kings

Another example of El Elyon showing up and revealing Himself as the exalted One who is victorious over all the so-called gods of this world is seen in the story of King Nebuchadnezzar in Daniel 4. Nebuchadnezzar was a great king with a vast empire, but eventually he began to regard himself as God.

Daniel 4:1 says, "Nebuchadnezzar the king [said] to all the peoples, nations, and men of every language that live in all the earth: 'May your peace abound!'" Nebuchadnezzar had become so big in his own head that he was blessing the people as if he was God. He seemed to have forgotten that El Elyon had made him king of Babylon.

Then one night King Nebuchadnezzar had a dream in which he saw a tree that grew as high as the sky. This tree was visible to the ends of the whole earth. Its foliage was beautiful, and its fruit was abundant—in it was enough food for all. The beasts of the field found shade under it, the birds dwelled in its branches, and all living creatures fed themselves from it.

In the dream, an angel of the Lord shouted from heaven for the tree to be chopped down, its branches cut off, and its fruit scattered. All that remained of the tree was a stump and its roots in the ground. The animals that rested under the tree and the birds that perched in its branches fled. Then the stump became drenched with the dew from heaven, and it was made to eat grass with the beasts of the earth for a period of seven years.

When King Nebuchadnezzar awoke from the dream, he was troubled and fearful. He called upon the wise men from Babylon to interpret his dream, but none could do so. Then King Nebuchadnezzar summoned the Hebrew prophet Daniel to interpret his dream. Daniel told Nebuchadnezzar that the king was the tree in the dream, and because of the king's pride, God would cut off his reign. King Nebuchadnezzar would be driven away from mankind to dwell among the beasts of the field, eating grass for seven years, until he recognized that El Elyon was the Most High God, the One who is sovereign over the entire earth.

Daniel pleaded with King Nebuchadnezzar to humble himself before God, but he refused. Twelve months later, as Nebuchadnezzar stood on the roof of his palace, he reflected on his power and glory, saying, "Is this not Babylon the great, which I myself have built as a royal residence by the might of my power and for the glory of *my* majesty?" (Dan. 4:30). While the words were still in his mouth, El Elyon showed up and told the king his sovereignty had been removed. The dream immediately came to pass, and Nebuchadnezzar began acting like an animal, eating grass like the cattle for seven years.

At the end of the seven years, God restored Nebuchadnezzar's senses and returned him to his throne. Now instead of exalting himself, the king blessed the one true God.

> But at the end of that period, I, Nebuchadnezzar, raised my eyes toward heaven and my reason returned to me, and I blessed the Most High [El Elyon] and praised and honored Him who lives forever; for His dominion is an everlasting dominion, and His kingdom endures from generation to generation. All the inhabitants of the earth are accounted as nothing, but He does according to His will in the host of heaven and among the inhabitants of earth; and no one can ward off His hand or say to Him, "What have You done?"
>
> At that time my reason returned to me. And my majesty and splendor were restored to me for the glory of my kingdom, and my counselors and my nobles began seeking me out; so I was reestablished in my sovereignty, and surpassing greatness was added to me. Now I, Nebuchadnezzar, praise, exalt and honor the King of

> heaven, for all His works are true and His ways just, and
> He is able to humble those who walk in pride.
>   —Daniel 4:34–37

Once again, God showed up as El Elyon when He needed to subdue an enemy on earth and demonstrate that He is sovereign not just in heaven above but also here on the earth.

Many in the church today believe and claim that God would never cause anyone to suffer or that He is never responsible for something we would think of as bad. For example, many think God would never cause sickness, but what about when God caused leprosy to strike Miriam (Numbers 12)? Or what about when God caused serpents to bite the children of Israel in the wilderness because of their sin (Num. 21:6–9)? Or when He caused David's child to die (2 Sam. 12:16–20) or Korah and his company to be swallowed up by the earth (Num. 16:1–40)?

What about when He drowned all the Egyptians in the sea (Exod. 14:13–31) or caused King Nebuchadnezzar to go insane for seven years? What would we say to that today? Most people's theology does not have a grid for understanding Isaiah 45:7 (kjv), "I form the light, and create darkness: I make peace, and create evil: I the Lord do all these things." This concept is called in Hebrew *Adon Olam*, which means that God is Master of the world. As Nebuchadnezzar said in Daniel 4, "He does according to His will in the host of heaven and among the inhabitants of earth; and no one can ward off His hand or say to Him, 'What have You done?'" (v. 35).

Sovereign Even in the Midst of Darkness

Another example of God's sovereignty on earth is seen when Abram, whose name was changed to Abraham (meaning "father of a multitude") in Genesis 17:5, sent his servant to find a bride for his son Isaac. Abraham's servant prayed:

> O LORD, the God of my master Abraham, please grant me success today, and show lovingkindness to my master Abraham. Behold, I am standing by the spring, and the daughters of the men of the city are coming out to draw water; now may it be that the girl to whom I say, "Please let down your jar so that I may drink," and who answers, "Drink, and I will water your camels also"—may she be the one whom You have appointed for Your servant Isaac; and by this I will know that You have shown lovingkindness to my master.
>
> —GENESIS 24:12–14

Before Abraham's servant had finished praying, a girl named Rebekah said, "Drink, my lord" (Gen. 24:18). And after she gave him a drink, she said, "I will draw also for your camels until they have finished drinking" (Gen. 24:19). Rebekah's words were perfectly synchronized with the prayer of Abraham's servant, demonstrating God's sovereignty upon the earth.

As incredible and faith-building as this story is, it also exposes a dilemma. Often it's easy to believe God is sovereign in heaven, but it's much more difficult to believe He's sovereign here on earth, especially when we see so much violence, chaos, injustice, starvation, and sickness in the world. When we see all these terrible things happening, we become fearful that God isn't supreme over all the forces that influence our lives. But God desires to strengthen our confidence in Him so we can know He's not only sovereign in heaven and on earth, but He's sovereign over every single circumstance we will ever face.

How can God reign supreme when we see so much darkness in the world? God in His sovereignty has chosen to temporarily step back from His creation, allowing the god of this world (Satan) to have limited freedom. An example of this is that Satan "has blinded the minds of the unbelieving so that they might not see the light of the gospel of the glory of Christ, who is the image of God" (2 Cor. 4:4). If you are not in relationship with Yeshua, you are at the mercy of Satan, who does everything in his power to keep people from seeing the truth of the gospel and the glory of Messiah Jesus in order to take them into eternal darkness and separation from God.

Currently, God's sovereign reign upon the earth is not directly being manifested in some situations and circumstances. In other words, in heaven there's no sorrow, sickness, suffering, or pain. But that is not the reality we face on earth. Yeshua taught us to "pray, then, in this way: 'Our Father who is in heaven, hallowed be Your name. *Your kingdom come. Your will be done, on earth as it is in heaven*'" (Matt. 6:9–10).

When we pray in this way, we are praying for God's kingdom and His will to be done on earth—and in our lives, families, and circumstances—as it is in heaven. We are asking for the power of heaven to reign in our lives while we are here on planet Earth. And as you keep seeking God and His righteousness above all else, He will invade your life and bless you.

This is what David was talking about in Psalm 91. He said:

He who dwells in the shelter of the Most High [El Elyon] will abide in the shadow of the Almighty. I will say to the LORD, "My refuge and my fortress, my God, in whom I trust!" For it is He who delivers you from the snare of the trapper and from the deadly pestilence. He will cover you with His pinions, and under His wings you may seek refuge; His faithfulness is a shield and bulwark.

—PSALM 91:1–4

When we abide under the shelter of El Elyon, God Most High, He is our refuge and our dwelling place, and no evil will come near us. Don't misunderstand. I am not saying that nothing bad will ever happen to you, but rather that even if we are faced with evil, we will have God's grace upon us in the midst of it.

Consider Stephen in Acts 7. After he had preached Jesus to his Jewish brethren, here is what happened:

Now when they heard this, they were cut to the quick, and they began gnashing their teeth at him. But being full of the Holy Spirit, he gazed intently into heaven and saw the glory of God, and Jesus standing at the right hand of God; and he said, "Behold, I see the heavens opened up and the Son of Man standing at the right hand of God." But they cried out with a loud voice, and covered their ears and rushed at him with one impulse. When they had driven him out of the city, they began stoning him; and the witnesses laid aside their robes at the feet of a young man named Saul. They went on stoning Stephen as he called on the Lord and said, "Lord Jesus, receive my spirit!" Then falling on his knees, he cried out with a loud voice, "Lord, do not hold this sin against them!" Having said this, he fell asleep.

—ACTS 7:54–60

Stephen is being stoned to death, but in the midst of it, he is covered with God's glory and has love flowing from his heart.

Psalm 91 goes on to say:

> You will not be afraid of the terror by night, or of the arrow that flies by day; of the pestilence that stalks in darkness, or of the destruction that lays waste at noon. A thousand may fall at your side and ten thousand at your right hand, but it shall not approach you. You will only look on with your eyes and see the recompense of the wicked. For you have made the LORD, my refuge, even the Most High [El Elyon], your dwelling place. No evil will befall you, nor will any plague come near your tent.
>
> For He will give His angels charge concerning you, to guard you in all your ways. They will bear you up in their hands, that you do not strike your foot against a stone. You will tread upon the lion and cobra, the young lion and the serpent you will trample down. "Because he has loved Me, therefore I will deliver him; I will set him securely on high, because he has known My name. He will call upon Me, and I will answer him; I will be with him in trouble; I will rescue him and honor him. With a long life I will satisfy him and let him see My salvation."
>
> —PSALM 91:5–16

The point is God is sovereign, and He desires to bring us to a place where we are confident of this reality and trust in His love so we have no fear. The Bible says, "There is no fear in love; but perfect love casts out fear" (1 John 4:18).

As I mentioned previously, El Elyon parted the Red Sea for the children of Israel to travel across (Exod. 14). He also opened the earth and swallowed up Korah and the others who rebelled against Moses (Num. 16). God will exercise

His direct sovereignty upon this earth when He desires, and He'll do the same for you when you seek Him.

The time is soon coming when God will take full possession of the earth, reigning upon it as El Elyon. We read about this in the Book of Revelation:

> Then the seventh angel sounded; and there were loud voices in heaven, saying, "The kingdom of the world has become the kingdom of our Lord and of His Christ [Messiah]; and He will reign forever and ever." And the twenty-four elders, who sit on their thrones before God, fell on their faces and worshiped God, saying, "We give You thanks, O Lord God, the Almighty, who are and who were, because You have taken Your great power and have begun to reign."
>
> —REVELATION 11:15–17

At this present time, El Elyon has stepped back a bit, allowing certain events to take place on the earth. But a time is coming when God Most High will break the power of Satan and destroy evil forever. Then El Elyon's fullness will cover the entire earth, as the waters cover the sea (Hab. 2:14), and He will reign on earth forever and ever, and there will no longer be any death, mourning, crying, or pain. Hallelujah!

John paints a vivid picture of what it will be like when Messiah begins to reign.

> And I heard a loud voice from the throne, saying, "Behold, the tabernacle of God is among men, and He will dwell among them, and they shall be His people, and God Himself will be among them, and He will wipe away every tear from their eyes; and there will no longer

be any death; there will no longer be any mourning, or
crying, or pain; the first things have passed away."
—REVELATION 21:3–4

Beloved, as we're waiting for this time to come, we must
have faith that even though at times things may seem to be
falling apart, it doesn't have to be that way for us if we make
El Elyon the Lord of our hearts. The Bible admonishes us
to "know therefore today, and take it to your heart, that the
LORD, He is God in heaven above and on the earth below;
there is no other" (Deut. 4:39).

Whatever problem you may be facing, you can be confident that El Elyon is completely sovereign over it because
He is supreme over every situation and circumstance in
your life. He is the highest authority there is—greater than
every problem, diagnosis, or financial difficulty you may
face. Trust El Elyon to reign in your life. Abide in Him,
cling to Him, completely depend upon Him, and He will
be your victory.

CHAPTER 3

EL SHADDAI—GOD ALMIGHTY

THROUGHOUT THE SCRIPTURES, when God revealed Himself to mankind, He did so in ways that directly correspond to the specific needs we have. This is true of when God revealed Himself as El Shaddai. He made Himself known as "God Almighty" in response to Abraham's deep need.

In Genesis 15, God made a promise to Abraham, who was still called Abram at the time. Although Abram and his wife were childless, God "took him outside and said, 'Now look toward the heavens, and count the stars, if you are able to count them....So shall your descendants be'" (v. 5). We can only imagine how it must have made Abram feel to hear that his offspring would be as numerous as the stars, which can hardly be counted, when as yet he hadn't been able to conceive one child with his wife. Only a powerful God could have made such a promise and kept it.

Yet after living in the land of Canaan for ten years, Abram still did not have any children because his wife, Sarai, was unable to give birth. After waiting so long for God to fulfill His promise, Abram and Sarai thought they should take matters into their own hands.

> Now Sarai, Abram's wife, had borne him no children, and she had an Egyptian maid whose name was Hagar. So Sarai said to Abram, "Now behold, the LORD has prevented me from bearing children. Please go in to my maid; perhaps I will obtain children through her." And Abram listened to the voice of Sarai. After Abram had lived ten years in the land of Canaan, Abram's wife Sarai took Hagar the Egyptian, her maid, and gave her to her husband Abram as his wife. He went in to Hagar, and she conceived....So Hagar bore Abram a son; and Abram called the name of his son, whom Hagar bore, Ishmael. Abram was eighty-six years old when Hagar bore Ishmael to him.
>
> —GENESIS 16:1–4, 15–16

But Ishmael was not the child God promised, so when Abram was ninety-nine years old, God appeared to him again and said, "I am God Almighty [El Shaddai]...and I will multiply you exceedingly" (Gen. 17:1–2).

The Scriptures say Abram fell on his face, and God went on to say:

> "As for Me, behold, My covenant is with you, and you will be the father of a multitude of nations. No longer shall your name be called Abram, but your name shall be Abraham; for I have made you the father of a multitude of nations."...Then God said to Abraham, "As for Sarai your wife, you shall not call her name Sarai, but Sarah shall be her name. I will bless her, and indeed I will give you a son by her. Then I will bless her, and she shall be a mother of nations; kings of peoples will come from her."

Then Abraham...laughed, and said in his heart, "Will a child be born to a man one hundred years old? And will Sarah, who is ninety years old, bear a child?" And Abraham said to God, "Oh that Ishmael might live before You!" But God said, "No, but Sarah your wife will bear you a son, and you shall call his name Isaac; and I will establish My covenant with him for an everlasting covenant for his descendants after him."

—GENESIS 17:3–5, 15–19

In response to Abraham's need for a son through his barren wife, Sarah, God revealed Himself as El Shaddai, "God Almighty," the One who is able to do anything.

And the LORD said to Abraham..."Is anything too difficult for the LORD? At the appointed time I will return to you, at this time next year, and Sarah will have a son."

—GENESIS 18:13–14

What was impossible for Abraham in the natural would now be fulfilled in the supernatural through the One who is almighty, the One for whom nothing is impossible. Despite being far beyond childbearing age, Sarah gave birth to a son they named Isaac, and the everlasting covenant God inaugurated with Abraham was established through Isaac and his descendants.

El Shaddai Meets Our Needs

El Shaddai met Abraham's need supernaturally, and He does the same for you and me today. God reveals His character through His names, and in the name El Shaddai, God reveals Himself as the almighty God who is able to meet every need.

As we discussed previously, *El* is the Hebrew word for "God," and *Shaddai* comes from the Hebrew word *shad*, which means "breast," particularly a mother's breast.[1] So when God revealed Himself to Abraham as El Shaddai, He was telling Abraham that his need would be met as an infant's need is met through his mother's breast. By revealing Himself to Abraham as El Shaddai, God was saying in essence, "Abraham, I realize you don't understand how you could have a son at a hundred years old, but I am El Shaddai. I am God Almighty, and My power is sufficient to meet all human needs."

Perhaps you can relate. Maybe you have a financial need or feel God calling you to a particular purpose and don't see a way it can be accomplished in the natural. We must remember that El Shaddai is God Almighty. He can do anything, even what seems impossible to us, and we can trust Him to fulfill the specific destinies to which He has called each of us. One of my favorite passages of the Bible is found in the Book of Numbers, which recounts the story of Moses doubting God's ability to feed the six hundred thousand Israelites who traveled with him.

> But Moses said, "The people, among whom I am, are 600,000 on foot; yet You have said, 'I will give them meat, so that they may eat for a whole month.' Should flocks and herds be slaughtered for them, to be sufficient for them? Or should all the fish of the sea be gathered together for them, to be sufficient for them?" The LORD said to Moses, "Is the LORD's power limited?"
> —NUMBERS 11:21–23

Now, I want to provide balance here. There is a lot of hype in the church today, with people thinking God is going to give them all their desires. We shouldn't expect God to provide us with something simply because we desire it. That isn't biblical. God hasn't promised us the American dream. What God has promised is that we would know Him and have peace, joy, and fullness in Him. El Shaddai will supply the needs that are in accordance with His will. He will fulfill the destiny He has called us to. God isn't interested in pampering our flesh. He won't give us what we want just because we want it. God provides for what *He* orders.

It wasn't Abraham's idea to become the father of many nations, and it wasn't his idea to have a child at a hundred years old; it was God's. And because it was God's will for Abraham, He supplied all that was needed to bring His promise to fulfillment. El Shaddai—God Almighty—will do the same in your life. He will work supernaturally to accomplish in and through you all that He has purposed for you.

I've seen this happen in my own life. Many years ago, I was leading a small Messianic congregation that met in a sanctuary we were renting that was about 35 feet by 70 feet. We maxed out our capacity with only fifty people in the building, but we didn't have enough money to buy a larger facility. Even though the building was small, I thought we should buy the property because it sat on three acres we could eventually build on.

I signed the contract to buy the facility, and soon afterward I had a dream. In the dream, I saw a person opening a health food store in an old, run-down residential neighborhood. On top of that, the health food store was on the second story of the only commercial building in this residential area. There was no commercial traffic in the neighborhood; in fact, the only people who traveled down the street were those who lived there. As I watched this man opening up this health food store in my dream, I said, "This man isn't going to succeed. He's in the wrong location." Then I woke up.

Because God often speaks to me in dreams, I sought the Lord to understand what the dream meant. A short while later, it occurred to me that I'm in the health business. I don't sell vitamins, but Yeshua Himself, Yahweh Ropheka, is our healer. Then all of a sudden the Lord showed me that the dream of the man opening a health food store in the wrong location was symbolic of me purchasing the building we were meeting in. Just like the building in the dream, our facility was located on an old residential street where there were no commercial buildings. The building was in the wrong location for our congregation long-term.

I felt the Lord was using the dream to show me that if I purchased that facility, my ministry would not succeed, but I didn't know what to do because I had already signed the contract to purchase the building. Yet at the very last minute, because our congregation was very small and our finances quite limited, I had given up hope of finding an adequate location for our needs. I had looked everywhere throughout our city, but nothing that was suitable was in our price range. So like Abraham, who had abandoned hope of bearing a son through his own wife, Sarai, and went in to Hagar, I signed a contract on a building that wasn't right. But El Shaddai stepped in. Through supernatural means, the Lord not only released me from the contract, but He provided a facility for our congregation that we never saw coming.

When our congregation was in need of a building, I did everything I could, but I reached a point where I had done all I could do. Then El Shaddai showed up. He was El Shaddai for Abraham, He was El Shaddai for me, and He is El Shaddai for all His children! The Lord wants our faith to be rooted in Him and in the supernatural.

El Shaddai's Covenant With Abraham Fulfilled in Yeshua

Later, El Shaddai also promised Abraham, "In your seed all the nations of the earth shall be blessed" (Gen. 22:18). Notice the word *seed* in this verse is singular, implying just *one* person. When God told Abraham that in his *seed* the nations of the earth would be blessed, the *seed* He was referring to was Yeshua.

Paul specifically details this point in Galatians 3:16: "Now the promises were spoken to Abraham and to his seed. He does not say, 'And to seeds,' as referring to many, but rather to one, 'And to your seed,' that is, Christ [Messiah]." In fact, the New Testament opens up with these words: "The record of the genealogy of Jesus the Messiah, the son of David, the son of Abraham" (Matt. 1:1).

The new covenant inaugurated at Passover with Yeshua's blood is the fulfillment of the covenant El Shaddai made with Abraham to bless all the nations of the earth through his seed:

> And when He had taken a cup and given thanks, He gave it to them, saying, "Drink from it, all of you; for this is My blood of the covenant, which is poured out for *many* for forgiveness of sins."
>
> —MATTHEW 26:27–28

Through Messiah Yeshua, the blessing that was upon Abraham's life is now upon you (Gal. 3:14).

Trust El Shaddai

When God told Abraham he would have a son through Sarah, Abraham laughed. It was easier for Abraham to believe God could bless Ishmael than it was for him to believe God could supernaturally give him a son through his wife, who was ninety years old.

We must trust that El Shaddai will supernaturally meet our needs, and when we do, we will walk in His abundance and blessing. As the apostle Paul wrote, "And my God will supply all your needs according to His riches in glory in [Messiah] Jesus" (Phil. 4:19).

If you desire to walk with the God who spoke to Abraham, then you must fully trust Him and His leading through the Holy Spirit, the Ruach HaKodesh. Abraham is the father of all who believe because he entered into relationship with God through his faith, just as we do today, both Jew and Gentile alike. (See Romans 4.)

Even though Abraham was a great man of faith, he lived a life like ours, walking partly in the flesh and partly in faith. When Abraham lived in the flesh, failing to trust in El Shaddai's supernatural power, the result was failure to enter into the fullness of his inheritance. The descendants of Hagar's son, Ishmael, have been a source of contention for the Jewish people for centuries, even until today.

When we live in the flesh, as Abraham did when he sought to bring God's promise to pass through his own works, nothing good will come from it. We must learn to cease our efforts and allow El Shaddai to supernaturally meet our needs.

So I want to encourage you to step out in faith, trusting El Shaddai to supernaturally perform His will in and through you. Rather than attempting to accomplish things in your own ability, begin sitting before God Almighty, spending time with Him and developing a sensitivity to the leading of His Spirit. When we commit to following and trusting Him in faith, El Shaddai will supernaturally meet our need, just as an infant's need is met through his mother's breast.

PART II

THE COVENANT NAMES OF GOD

CHAPTER 4

YAHWEH—GOD'S PERSONAL NAME

As we have seen in the previous chapters, God revealed Himself to Abraham, Isaac, and Jacob as Elohim (God the Creator), El Elyon (God Most High), and El Shaddai (God Almighty). But in the Book of Exodus (Shemot), God goes further and reveals Himself to Moses by His name, Yahweh.

> God spoke further to Moses and said to him, "I am the LORD [Yahweh]; and I appeared to Abraham, Isaac, and Jacob, as God Almighty [El Shaddai], but by My name, LORD [Yahweh], I did not make Myself known to them."
>
> —EXODUS 6:2–3

Yahweh—comprised of the Hebrew consonants *yod*, *hey*, *vav*, *hey*—is God's sacred, personal name. Moses Maimonides, one of the most famous Jewish sages in history, said Yahweh is the only true name of God mentioned in Scripture; all the others are titles because they are derived from His works. *Elohim*, for example, describes God as the

Creator, and *El Shaddai* describes Him as God Almighty, but He has only one name, and that name is Yahweh. It is much like it is with you and me. You could call me a rabbi, a husband, a father, or a son, but these are titles based on what I do. I have only one name, and that is Kirt Schneider.

There's something personal about knowing someone by name. If you call a person just by his title, there's a sense of disconnectedness. But when you learn someone's name and begin to call him lovingly and respectfully by it, a personal relationship is formed.

This is what God wants. Elohim created us in His very own image, and His greatest desire is to have fellowship with us. He wants us to feel comfortable enough with Him to call upon Him by His name. Many times when people think about God, they think He is very far away. But in revealing His personal name, the Creator of the universe is letting us know He's a real person who loves us and longs to be close to us.

After God made Himself known as Yahweh, everyone in the Old Testament from Moses onward called upon Father God in love and reverence by His personal name. In fact, God's covenant name is used nearly seven thousand times in Scripture.

In every place in the Old Testament where we see the word LORD in capital letters, it is actually the Hebrew consonants *yod, hey, vav, hey* (YHWH), which is God's personal name, Yahweh. Bible translators actually have done us a disservice and obscured the truth by translating God's name simply as LORD because the word *Lord* is a title describing God as a ruler. When we read the word LORD rather than God's name, Yahweh, the personal dimension of the revelation

God desires to impart is taken away. Yahweh revealed His personal name to us so we could know His love for us, the love of a real person.

In giving us His personal name, God is showing us that He's not simply a force or "energy"; He's a person who loves us and wants a personal relationship with us. He desires intimacy with us. He wants us to know Him by name, call upon Him by name, and trust Him through His names.

Yahweh—the I Am

The name Yahweh is brought into full view in Exodus chapter 3, where Moses encounters the burning bush. God appears to Moses in a fire coming from a bush that wasn't being consumed by the blaze. And He tells Moses He's going to send him to Pharaoh to deliver the Israelites out of Egypt and lead them to the Promised Land, a land flowing with milk and honey. Moses then asks God who he should say has sent him.

> God said to Moses, "I Am Who I Am"; and He said, "Thus you shall say to the sons of Israel, 'I Am has sent me to you.'" God, furthermore, said to Moses, "Thus you shall say to the sons of Israel, 'The LORD [Yahweh], the God of your fathers, the God of Abraham, the God of Isaac, and the God of Jacob, has sent me to you.' This is My name forever, and this is My memorial-name to all generations."
> —EXODUS 3:14–15

When God revealed His personal name to Moses and told him "I Am Who I Am," He was declaring that His presence would continually be with him forever. *Just as it was for Moses, so it is for you and me.* Yahweh is the ground of all being, and He is always present. He was present yesterday,

He's present right now, and He's going to be present for us in the future. He is the great I Am!

That knowledge should empower us to face the future without dread. Instead of imagining all the ways things can go wrong in the days ahead, we can declare by faith, "I Am is here." If we take hold of this revelation and stop thinking we have to face the future on our own, we'll be confident and victorious through all the challenges life brings because we'll know Yahweh is with us in the midst of them—today, tomorrow, and always.

Isaiah prophesied that Yeshua would be called Immanuel, which literally means, "With us is God." (See Isaiah 7:14 and Matthew 1:23.) When we understand that Yahweh is always with us, regardless of where we are or what we're going through, we will be able to face any difficulty that comes in our lives with strength because we'll know we won't be facing it alone.

Yahweh, the "I Am Who I Am," wants us to exercise faith in the darkness and declare that He's with us. Even when we don't feel His presence, we can take hold of His present reality through His name by faith and declare, "I Am is here." The Bible says, "The Lord [Yahweh] is the one who goes ahead of you; He will be with you. He will not fail you or forsake you. Do not fear or be dismayed" (Deut. 31:8). As we press in by faith and war against the lies of the enemy that would cause us to think God is not with us, we'll be led into His light and glory.

Yeshua Is Also the I Am

Yahweh is not only the great I Am; He is also our Savior. He declared in Isaiah 43:10–11:

"You are My witnesses," declares the LORD [Yahweh],
"and My servant whom I have chosen, so that you may
know and believe Me and understand that I am He.
Before Me there was no God formed, and there will be
none after Me. I, even I, am the LORD [Yahweh], and
there is no savior besides Me."

Just as Yahweh made Himself known as the great I Am,
so Yeshua, the visible manifestation of the invisible Yahweh,
used the phrase "I am" to refer to Himself. He told His disciples, "Truly, truly, I say to you, before Abraham was born,
I am" (John 8:58).

The Gospel of John records Yeshua making seven "I am"
statements:

1. "I am the bread of life" (John 6:35).

2. "I am the Light of the world" (John 8:12).

3. "I am the door" (John 10:9).

4. "I am the good shepherd" (John 10:11).

5. "I am the resurrection and the life" (John 11:25).

6. "I am the way, and the truth, and the life"
   (John 14:6).

7. "I am the true vine" (John 15:1).

There is only one reason Yeshua uses such similar language. It's because He is God in the flesh.

Yahweh Has Likes and Dislikes

Yahweh is a real person who sees us, hears us, has thoughts
toward us, and feels things. He has likes and dislikes, just as

you and I do. Scripture tells us Yahweh loves humility, sincerity, truthfulness, intimate relationships, and faithfulness, but there are also things He hates.

> There are six things which the LORD [Yahweh] hates, yes, seven which are an abomination to Him: haughty eyes, a lying tongue, and hands that shed innocent blood, a heart that devises wicked plans, feet that run rapidly to evil, a false witness who utters lies, and one who spreads strife among brothers.
>
> —PROVERBS 6:16–19

I want to briefly look at each one.

1. Haughty eyes. When people have haughty eyes, they have a condescending spirit and look upon others with contempt. In His parable in Luke 18 about the Pharisee and the tax collector who went into the Temple to pray, Yeshua made it clear that the tax collector and not the Pharisee went home justified because the tax collector humbled himself before God while the Pharisee had haughty eyes, was prideful, and viewed others with contempt. We must take care to be kind, gracious, and humble toward others, especially those who don't have the same advantages we have or who have physical or mental disabilities. We are to love others as Yahweh loves them. He doesn't want us to consider ourselves better than anyone else.

2. A lying tongue. It's amazing how many of God's people are habitual liars and don't think anything of it or are not even aware of their behavior. Many people lie because they are afraid of the consequences of telling the truth. The Scriptures tell us that God cannot lie; He is truth and light, and in Him there is no darkness at all (Num. 23:19; 1 John

5:1). By having a commitment of not lying, I have found that God always gives me the wisdom to know how to respond in difficult situations.

3. Hands that shed innocent blood. This obviously means taking advantage of innocent people. We see this happening all the time in the business world. People prey on others for their own financial gain. We must be careful how we treat others—our thoughts, words, and actions toward them—because God will judge us.

4. A heart that devises wicked plans. Some people are so trapped in negativity that they constantly think of ways in which they can stir up a situation. Think of the media and the way some outlets spin stories and create a false narrative to advance their own wicked agendas. Yahweh hates this.

5. Feet that rapidly run to evil. I believe many Christians are trapped in this when we constantly complain or continually criticize. Scripture tells us, "Whatever is true, whatever is honorable, whatever is right, whatever is pure, whatever is lovely, whatever is of good repute, if there is any excellence and if anything worthy of praise, dwell on these things" (Phil. 4:8).

It's easy to complain and criticize, but we must discipline ourselves to resist this spirit. We must reserve our tongues for praising and blessing others. When our conversations are pleasing to Yahweh, we will overcome evil with good and ascend in the light.

6. A false witness who utters lies. This is a person who intentionally gossips and speaks untruths about others. Our words must be continually spoken in truthfulness.

7. Spreading strife among others. This usually occurs in individuals who are caught in the negativism of running swiftly to evil. These people are constantly complaining, criticizing, and talking behind people's backs. We must guard against spreading strife. Be one who preserves the bond of peace, unity, and love.

Beloved one, if we want to draw close to Yahweh, we **must love what He loves and hate what He hates.**

Yahweh Is Jealous

As we continue to uncover Yahweh's personality, let us also consider that God is jealous for us:

> Then God spoke all these words, saying, "I am the Lord [Yahweh] your God, who brought you out of the land of Egypt, out of the house of slavery. You shall have no other gods before Me. You shall not make for yourself an idol, or any likeness of what is in heaven above or on the earth beneath or in the water under the earth. You shall not worship them or serve them; for I, the Lord [Yahweh] your God, am a *jealous* God."
> —Exodus 20:1–5

> You shall not worship any other god, for the Lord [Yahweh], whose name is *Jealous*, is a *jealous* God.
> —Exodus 34:14

Elohim created us in His own image for Himself. He is jealous when people and things have greater importance in our lives than He does.

Yahweh is also jealous when we live primarily to please ourselves rather than asking Him each day, "What can I do today, God, to please You?" or, "What can I do to bring myself under Your subjection?" or, "What can I do to walk in victory with You by denying myself? Help me to come under greater subjection to Your Son, Your Word, and Your lordship in my life. Bring me into alignment with You."

Remember, Messiah Jesus said, "If anyone wishes to come after Me, he must deny himself, and take up his cross and follow Me" (Matt. 16:24). We must be totally committed to Yahweh, denying ourselves and putting Him first.

This is how Yeshua lived His life. He didn't want to endure the pain of the cross, yet He told the Father, "Not My will, but Yours be done" (Luke 22:41–42). If we spend our lives doing what we want, seeking our own pleasures, we will fail in the end. Yeshua said, "Whoever wishes to save his life will lose it; but whoever loses his life for My sake will find it" (Matt. 16:25–26).

If we put our own pleasures first, making decisions based only on what we want and like, then we're not truly living for Yahweh. He is jealous, and unless we give ourselves totally to Him, we will forfeit our very souls. "For what does it profit a man to gain the whole world, and forfeit his soul?" (Mark 8:36).

Yahweh Hurts and Weeps

You see, Yahweh is a real person who has emotions just like you and me. He hurts, grieves, and even weeps.

We read in Genesis 6:6 that "the LORD [Yahweh] was sorry that He had made man on the earth, and He was grieved in His heart." Sometimes we fail to understand that we can literally hurt God. You might ask, "How can I hurt and grieve God? He's so powerful." If you're a parent, you've likely been hurt and grieved by your child. Even though you have absolute power over your infant child and then, as they mature, the power to correct and punish them, they can hurt and grieve you by their words and actions. It's the same with Yahweh. Even though He is all-powerful, He's also sensitive and can be hurt and grieved by our words and actions.

So again, I make the point that Yahweh has emotions. We see this in the life of Yeshua, who is Yahweh in the flesh. He wept when Mary and Martha's brother Lazarus died (John 11:35). Just as we sometimes express our inner emotions with tears, so too did Yeshua as He wept for Lazarus.

Consider that Yahweh also thinks about us. The psalmist says, "How precious also are Your thoughts to me, O God! How vast is the sum of them! If I should count them, they would outnumber the sand" (Ps. 139:17–18). Isn't it incredible to know Yahweh thinks about us and has precious thoughts of love toward us?

Beloved, Yahweh wants you to know Him as a person. He wants you to know who He is and what He likes and dislikes so you can conform yourself to His life and become like Him. In doing so, you will grow in intimacy with Him and fulfill the purpose for which you were created.

Yahweh Is Constantly Moving

Yahweh is a living person who exists in the state of continuous unfinished action. We see this expressed in Isaiah 6 and Revelation 4, which describe the scene around His throne. Day and night the angelic beings never cease crying, "Holy, holy, holy."

> In the year of King Uzziah's death I saw the Lord sitting on a throne, lofty and exalted, with the train of His robe filling the temple. Seraphim stood above Him, each having six wings: with two he covered his face, and with two he covered his feet, and with two he flew. And one

called out to another and said, "Holy, Holy, Holy, is the LORD of hosts, the whole earth is full of His glory."

—ISAIAH 6:1–3

And the four living creatures, each one of them having six wings, are full of eyes around and within; and day and night they do not cease to say, "Holy, holy, holy is the LORD God, the Almighty, who was and who is and who is to come."

—REVELATION 4:8

The angelic beings continuously cry "Holy, Holy, Holy" because new emanations of God's holiness and glory are constantly bubbling forth. Every time they see Him, they experience a new revelation of who He is. Each time they say "Holy," they are responding to a fresh, new unfolding manifestation of who He is.

Some people believe heaven will be a boring place, but nothing could be further from the truth. Yahweh wants you to know there is always more of Him to discover; He is continually fresh and brand new. You will never get bored of knowing God, and you will be forever drawn into a deeper, more intimate state of experiencing His presence and glory.

We Are Partakers in Covenants Guaranteed by Yahweh's Name

It's important for us to understand that the covenants in Scripture that you and I partake of have been given to us in God's personal name. God's covenants are more specifically Yahweh's covenants. For example, looking again at Exodus 6:2–4, we see that God said, "I am the LORD [Yahweh]; and I appeared to Abraham, Isaac, and Jacob, as God Almighty [El Shaddai], but by My name, LORD [Yahweh], I did not

make Myself known to them. *I also established My covenant with them, to give them the land of Canaan, the land
in which they sojourned.*"

So God established His covenant with Abraham, Isaac,
and Jacob in His name, Yahweh. We also see in Exodus 20,
in association with the giving of the Ten Commandments,
that God revealed Himself to Israel as "the LORD [Yahweh]
your God, who brought you out of the land of Egypt, out of
the house of slavery" (v. 2).

It was Yahweh who later made the promise of a new covenant with Israel, pledging to forgive their sin and place His
Spirit, the Ruach HaKodesh, within them.

> Moreover, I will give you a new heart and put a new
> spirit within you; and I will remove the heart of stone
> from your flesh and give you a heart of flesh. I will put
> My Spirit within you and cause you to walk in My stat-
> utes, and you will be careful to observe My ordinances.
> —Ezekiel 36:26–27

> "Behold, days are coming," declares the LORD [Yahweh],
> "when I will make a new covenant with the house of
> Israel and with the house of Judah, not like the covenant
> which I made with their fathers in the day I took them
> by the hand to bring them out of the land of Egypt, My
> covenant which they broke, although I was a husband to
> them," declares the LORD [Yahweh]. "But this is the cov-
> enant which I will make with the house of Israel after
> those days," declares the LORD [Yahweh], "I will put My
> law within them and on their heart I will write it; and I
> will be their God, and they shall be My people. They will
> not teach again, each man his neighbor and each man
> his brother, saying, 'Know the LORD [Yahweh],' for they
> will all know Me, from the least of them to the greatest

of them," declares the LORD [Yahweh], "for I will forgive
their iniquity, and their sin I will remember no more."
—JEREMIAH 31:31–34

Yeshua instituted this new covenant when He celebrated
Passover with His disciples before He was crucified. As He
lifted up the Passover wine, He proclaimed that His blood
would establish the basis on which the new covenant is
founded.

> And when He had taken a cup and given thanks, He
> gave it to them, saying, "Drink from it, all of you; for
> this is My blood of the covenant, which is poured out for
> many for forgiveness of sins."
> —MATTHEW 26:27–28

Jew and Gentile alike have been brought into a covenantal relationship with Yahweh.

It's such a blessing that the covenants God made in
Scripture are sealed with His personal name. Yahweh's name
upon the covenants guarantees them, giving us complete
confidence to trust in them. It isn't an abstract God who has
given us these covenants but the very person Yahweh, the
one true God.

The Book of Hebrews tells us that when Yahweh made
the promise to Abraham, since there was no one greater for
Yahweh to swear by, He swore by Himself (Heb. 6:13). God
promised Abraham that in his "seed" all the nations of the
earth, Jew and Gentile, would be blessed. The word *seed* is
singular, referring to just *one* person: Messiah Yeshua.

As the Bible tells us in Galatians, the blessing that was upon
Abraham is now upon you and me through Messiah Jesus:

> ...in order that in [Messiah] Jesus the blessing of Abraham might come to the Gentiles, so that we would receive the promise of the Spirit through faith.
> —Galatians 3:14

So the covenant relationship you have with God through Messiah Yeshua's blood was actually inaugurated with the covenant God made with Abraham in the name of Yahweh.

Beloved, I want you to know Yahweh is a real person, and He responds. The Lord saw Abraham's willingness to offer his only son, and He said, "Abraham, because you've offered up your only son, I will greatly bless you." Yahweh responded to Abraham's love and sacrifice, and He will respond to you.

Yeshua said to go into your closet and pray and fast secretly because Yahweh, your Father, will see you doing these things and respond by rewarding you (Matt. 6:6, 18). Our obedience, just like Abraham's, moves God, so if you want God to bless you, obey Him. We don't earn our salvation, but Yahweh responds to our love and devotion to Him.

Yahweh is alive, and He sees you. If you draw near to Him, He will draw near to you (Jas. 4:8). If you ask, you'll receive; if you seek, you'll find; and if you knock, the door will be opened (Matt. 7:7–8).

Yeshua said in John 14, "He who has My commandments and keeps them is the one who loves Me; and he who loves Me will be loved by My Father, and I will love him and will disclose Myself to him....If anyone loves Me, he will keep My word; and My Father will love him, and We will come to him and make Our abode with him" (vv. 21, 23).

As we respond in love and obedience to Yeshua, He'll respond to us by revealing His love and manifesting His presence.

Abide in Yahweh

Yahweh's presence was with Adam and Eve (Gen. 5:2), He was with Enoch and Noah (Gen. 5:24; 6:9), and He is with you and me through the Holy Spirit (Ruach HaKodesh), who dwells within us. This is the mystery of the gospel: "Christ [Messiah] in you, the hope of glory" (Col. 1:27).

Many of us spend our lives searching for God outside ourselves when His literal presence is within us. To sense Yahweh's presence in our lives, we must cut ourselves off from all the distractions of the world. Resist the allure of sensuality. When we remove these things from our lives, we'll be able to sense the presence of the Creator within us.

Yahweh told us that if we would come out from the world and be separate unto Him, He would receive us to Himself.

> For we are the temple of the living God; just as God said, "I will dwell in them and walk among them; and I will be their God, and they shall be My people. Therefore, come out from their midst and be separate," says the Lord. "And do not touch what is unclean; and I will welcome you. And I will be a father to you, and you shall be sons and daughters to Me," says the Lord Almighty.
> —2 CORINTHIANS 6:16–18

As you come out from the distractions of the world to be separate unto Yahweh, spending time sitting still in His presence, He will enable you to sense His Spirit inside you. Yahweh will teach you how to abide in Him, and as you do, you'll walk with Him, just as Enoch, Noah, and most of all, Yeshua did.

In the next chapter, we're going to learn even more about Yahweh's character and nature revealed in His name.

CHAPTER 5

YAHWEH—A REVELATION OF GOD'S CHARACTER

A LL THE NAMES of God found in Scripture are derived from His works except one: Yahweh. Through this name, God revealed the nature of His substance and personality clearly and unequivocally, and nowhere is that more evident than in Exodus 34:6–7. This is one of my favorite passages of Scripture because in it the Lord our God reveals who He is.

The Bible says in Exodus 33 that Moses wanted to know God and His ways, so he prayed, "Show me Your glory!" (v. 18). The Lord told Moses that no one could see Him and live, but He said, "I Myself will make all My goodness pass before you, and *will proclaim the name of the* LORD *before you*" (v. 19).

God was saying, "Moses, you can't see Me, but I'm going to make you know who I am by proclaiming My name to you." The Lord placed Moses in the cleft of the rock, covering him with His hand, and as He passed by, God gave Moses revelation of who He is through His name.

> Then the LORD [Yahweh] passed by in front of him
> and proclaimed, "The LORD [Yahweh], the LORD God
> [Yahweh El], compassionate and gracious, slow to anger,
> and abounding in lovingkindness and truth; who keeps
> lovingkindness for thousands, who forgives iniquity,
> transgression and sin; yet He will by no means leave the
> guilty unpunished, visiting the iniquity of fathers on
> the children and on the grandchildren to the third and
> fourth generations."
>
> —Exodus 34:6–7

Other than the incarnation of Messiah Jesus, this is the
most incredible revelation of the essence of God in the
entire Bible.

The Lord begins by proclaiming His name, "The LORD,
the LORD God," which is to say Yahweh, Yahweh El. Why
does God repeat His name? He does it for emphasis. The
revelation God is about to give is so solemn, He swears
to its truthfulness by His own name. Since all creation is
beneath Him and there is no one greater for Him to swear
by, He swears by Himself that what He is about to say can
be trusted. Then He begins to supernaturally reveal to
Moses who He is.

Yahweh Is Compassionate

The first revelation God gave Moses is that He is compassionate. Our English word *compassionate*, which means to
be sympathetic to others, doesn't fully convey the beauty
of who Yahweh is. The Hebrew word translated "compassionate" in Exodus 34:6 is *rachum* (or *raḥûm*). This term is
closely related to the Hebrew word for "womb" and reflects

the tenderness, devotion, and loyalty a mother has for her infant child.

Even though the Lord is referred to in the masculine, He also has feminine characteristics. God created both male and female in His image (Gen. 1:27) because within Him there is both the masculine and feminine. The word *El* is masculine, and it is appropriate for us to use masculine pronouns to refer to God, but it's significant that when He first reveals His heart to us in Exodus 34:6, He uses a term that paints a picture of a mother's tender love and devotion for her child.

When a young child falls down on a sidewalk and his knee is bruised and bleeding, whom does that child typically run to, his father or his mother? Generally, the child will run to his mother because she is the tenderhearted one. She is often the one who will wrap that child in her arms and tenderly comfort him. Isn't it awesome that our Creator relates to us in that same way? When we've fallen, the Lord desires for us to run to Him so He can wrap us in His arms and tenderly nurture us.

Not long ago I read a testimony about a very successful person who testified that his success in life was due to the unconditional love of his mother. The Master of the universe loves us with that kind of love, a love that shelters and protects us no matter what. He longs for us to find in Him a place of comfort, rest, and acceptance, just what the apostle John found in Messiah Jesus as he leaned his head on Yeshua's bosom during the Passover meal (John 13:23).

The Lord loves us with the same intimate, tender mercies a mother has for her child. Yeshua, who is God in the flesh, told the Jewish people He desired to gather them to Himself as a mother hen gathers her chicks under her wings.

> Jerusalem, Jerusalem, who kills the prophets and stones those who are sent to her! How often I wanted to gather your children together, the way a hen gathers her chicks under her wings, and you were unwilling.
>
> —Matthew 23:37

Just as a mother hen gathers her chicks in to be close to her, so the Lord desires to be close to us.

God doesn't want you to know Him only as a stern disciplinarian; He also wants you to know His tender affection for you. Many of us still have the need for a mother's love, and that need can be met in Yahweh. If you didn't get the love you needed from your mother, it's not too late. Our God can supply that love for you because He is compassionate. He is *rachum*, and He loves you with a mother's affection.

Yahweh Is Gracious

After revealing Himself to Moses as compassionate, Yahweh said He is gracious. The Hebrew word translated "gracious" in Exodus 34:6 is *chanun* (also *ḥannûn*), which means favor. It conveys the idea of Yahweh stooping down to an inferior person and showing kindness to him even though he does not deserve it. Father God chooses to extend this kindness simply out of His love for us, not because we deserve it.

Yahweh knows our weaknesses. He realizes we are but dust, yet He desires to be gracious to us simply because of His fondness for us. Too many people see God as harsh, but the truth is that He stoops down to where we are. He gets us. He sent Messiah Yeshua to this earth to die on the cross so we can be in fellowship with Him. That's how loving and gracious He is to us.

Yahweh Is Slow to Anger

The third revelation Yahweh gave Moses is that He is slow to anger. The Hebrew word translated "slow" is *'erek* (or *ārēk*), and the Hebrew word translated "anger" comes from the word *'apayim*.

It is interesting that *'apayim* is actually a plural form of the Hebrew word for *anger*. As we saw in chapter 1, adding -im to the end of a Hebrew word can actually do one of two things. It can make the word plural, or it can give the word emphasis. The -im at the end of *'apayim* can make it plural, so as to say Yahweh is *slow to angers* toward us, or it can add emphasis, so as to say Yahweh is *slow to anger to the utmost*.

Whether the *-im* makes the term plural or adds emphasis, the point is the same: Yahweh is very patient and long-suffering. God our Creator demonstrated this characteristic during Noah's day when He gave mankind 120 years, the time it took Noah to construct the ark, to repent of their sin before bringing the judgment of the flood upon them (1 Pet. 3:20).

Yahweh also demonstrated His slowness to anger when He gave the Amorites four hundred years to repent of their sin before giving their land to the descendants of Abraham.

> God said to Abram, "Know for certain that your descendants will be strangers in a land that is not theirs, where they will be enslaved and oppressed four hundred years....Then in the fourth generation they will return here, for the iniquity of the Amorite is not yet complete."
> —Genesis 15:13, 16

We all fall short of the high calling of God in Messiah Yeshua. Not one of us can say we're perfect. How many times every day do our thoughts wander from the Lord?

How often do we believe things that aren't true? The first commandment is to love the Lord our God with all our heart, soul, mind, and strength (Mark 12:30). But how often do we fall short of this?

Yet in all the different ways we miss the mark, Yahweh is slow to angers toward us. He doesn't just get mad all of a sudden. He's not waiting to strike us down at any offense. He is long-suffering. As King David, a man who made many mistakes but knew God, declared, Yahweh is "merciful and gracious, slow to anger and abundant in lovingkindness and truth" (Ps. 86:15).

Yahweh Is Abounding in Lovingkindness

The next revelation Yahweh gave Moses is that He is abounding in lovingkindness. The word translated "abounding" in Exodus 34:6 is *rab*, which means beyond measure, unlimited, and overflowing.

Yeshua said, "I came that they may have life, and have it abundantly" (John 10:10). This abundant life Yeshua came to give us is abounding (beyond measure, unlimited, and overflowing). Yahweh doesn't hold anything back; He gives us much more than we could ever imagine! One day we will come to the realization of this. "Things which eye has not seen and ear has not heard, and which have not entered the heart of man, all that God has prepared for those who love Him" (1 Cor. 2:9).

The Hebrew word translated "lovingkindness" is *chesed* (or *ḥesed*), which implies a faithful, unfailing covenant love. Yahweh is abounding in a faithful, unfailing covenant love for us. His love is loyal; He never leaves us nor forsakes us. He is committed, and His love is unconditional;

it isn't dependent upon our actions. Yahweh's love for us is abounding—it keeps coming and coming.

David spoke of Yahweh's lovingkindness, saying, "Surely goodness and *lovingkindness* will follow me all the days of my life, and I will dwell in the house of the LORD [Yahweh] forever" (Ps. 23:6). The psalmist also wrote, "Give thanks to the LORD [Yahweh], for He is good, for His *lovingkindness* is everlasting" (Ps. 136:1).

Yeshua proved Yahweh's abounding lovingkindness toward us when He died on the cross for our sins.

Yahweh Is Abounding in Truth

Exodus 34:6 says Yahweh is abounding not only in *lovingkindness* but also in *truth*. It is really interesting that in Scripture we often see lovingkindness (*chesed*) married or coupled with truth (*'ĕmet*). It's clear these two go hand in hand.

> *Lovingkindness* and *truth* have met together.
> —PSALM 85:10

> Righteousness and justice are the foundation of Your throne; *lovingkindness* and *truth* go before You.
> —PSALM 89:14

> You, O LORD [Yahweh], will not withhold Your compassion from me; Your *lovingkindness* and Your *truth* will continually preserve me.
> —PSALM 40:11

It is no accident that Scripture says, "The Word became flesh, and dwelt among us, and we saw His glory, glory as of the only begotten from the Father, *full of grace and truth*" (John 1:14). Messiah Jesus is the *visible manifestation* of the

One who is "abounding in lovingkindness and truth" (Exod. 34:6). Because Yeshua is Yahweh incarnate, He too is full of grace (or lovingkindness) and truth.

Yahweh Is Forgiving

God is not only compassionate, gracious, slow to anger, and abounding in lovingkindness and truth, but He also forgives our sin whenever we turn to Him with a repentant heart.

The Hebrew word translated "forgives" in Exodus 34:7 is *nāśā'*, and it means to cast, wipe away, and pardon our sins. Beloved, Yahweh doesn't hold our sin over our heads. In His compassion and lovingkindness He sent Yeshua, the sinless Lamb of God, to die on the cross. Through this sacrifice, our sin was transferred into Yeshua Messiah, and He carried our sin away as far as the east is from the west, so we can stand righteous before God. "If we confess our sins, He is faithful and righteous to forgive us our sins and to cleanse us from all unrighteousness" (1 John 1:9).

Whenever you begin to question whether God has truly forgiven you, remember what He said in His Word.

> As far as the east is from the west, so far has He removed our transgressions from us.
>
> —Psalm 103:12

> He made Him who knew no sin to be sin on our behalf, so that we might become the righteousness of God in Him.
>
> —2 Corinthians 5:21

Yahweh is not a God who is mad. He's glad! He is able to show us affection, favor, and forgiveness because Yeshua has set us free from the bondage of sin and death and given us the free gift of salvation (Rom. 6:23). The devil wants to accuse us of sins that have already been forgiven. You and I must remember that Messiah Jesus has paid the price for our transgressions, and He has set us free.

Yahweh Will Not Leave the Guilty Unpunished

Beloved, we also need to know that although our Lord is compassionate, gracious, and longsuffering, those who refuse to repent and receive His free gift of forgiveness will be judged. Yahweh revealed to Moses that *"He will by no means leave the guilty unpunished"* (Exod. 34:7). He will eventually bring justice to those who have turned their backs on Him.

Yahweh is a God of justice, and He will destroy from the face of the earth those who refuse to receive Yeshua, who died in their place, and repent of their sin. As it was in the days of Noah when the Creator destroyed everyone who wouldn't turn to Him, humble themselves, and repent, so it will be at the end of the age. One day those who have continually rejected Yeshua's free gift of salvation will have to stand before Him to pay the penalty for their sin. Those whose names are not written in the Lamb's Book of Life will be thrown into hell and the lake of fire (Rev. 20:15). Meanwhile, those who have received Yeshua's payment for their sin will live forever in the glorious, blissful, majestic presence of God.

The last chapter of Revelation paints a vivid picture of the glorious future that awaits those who put their trust in God through Messiah Yeshua:

Then he showed me a river of the water of life, clear as crystal, coming from the throne of God and of the Lamb, in the middle of its street. On either side of the river was the tree of life, bearing twelve kinds of fruit, yielding its fruit every month; and the leaves of the tree were for the healing of the nations. There will no longer be any curse; and the throne of God and of the Lamb will be in it, and His bond-servants will serve Him; they will see His face, and His name will be on their foreheads. And there will no longer be any night; and they will not have need of the light of a lamp nor the light of the sun, because the Lord God will illumine them; and they will reign forever and ever.

—Revelation 22:1–5

Yahweh is preparing things for us that are beyond anything we could ever comprehend.

Yeshua Is the Exact Representation of Yahweh

When we accept Yeshua, we are accepting Yahweh because all the characteristics of Yahweh revealed in Exodus 34 are embodied in Messiah Jesus, who said, "He who has seen Me has seen the Father" (John 14:9).

Yeshua is compassionate, gracious, slow to anger, abounding in lovingkindness, abounding in truth, forgiving of our sin, and a just God who doesn't leave the guilty unpunished. When we pray to Yeshua, we are praying to the same God revealed to us in Exodus 34.

If you allow this revelation of Yahweh to truly sink deep into your heart, you will come to know Him as a compassionate God who loves you with the tender affection of a mother for her child. You will know Him as your gracious

Lord who releases His favor and kindness upon and into your life. You will experience Him as slow to anger and long-suffering toward you. You will become confident of His lovingkindness and abounding, faithful, covenant love. All of this will bring freedom into your life.

A Name Meant to Be Spoken

In Exodus 3:15, when God first introduces Himself as Yahweh, He says, "This is My name forever, and *this is My memorial-name to all generations.*" It is God's desire for us today to not only know His personal name, Yahweh, but to call upon His name throughout all our generations.

Today most Jewish people do not speak God's name, Yahweh. There are several reasons for this, but the main one is that as time unfolded in history, the Hebrew nation began to feel that God's personal name was so sacred it shouldn't be uttered. They feared that if the heathen nations found out His name, they would profane it. By Messiah Yeshua's day, the only people using God's covenant name, Yahweh, were the priests in the Temple.

When the Temple was destroyed in AD 70 and the priesthood was scattered, the Jewish community stopped using the name Yahweh altogether, and since that time, it has not been common to use God's sacred, personal name. In fact, today in Orthodox Judaism, the name Yahweh is deemed so sacred it is considered sacrilegious to speak it. Instead of saying Yahweh, Orthodox Jews will say "HaShem," a Hebrew word meaning "The Name." Or they will use the Hebrew term *Adonai*, which means "Lord."

I think it's wonderful that within Judaism, God's name is so reverenced they won't even utter it. But as beautiful as that tradition is, it's not biblical. The reason God referred to Himself by His name, Yahweh, almost seven thousand times in the Hebrew Bible is so His people would use it to call upon Him. It is important that we can know the Lord by His name. Calling upon Him in reverence and love by His name brings us into greater intimacy with Him and helps us better understand Him as our Father. By knowing God's name, we come to know Him not as an abstract concept but as a living person.

All throughout the Old Testament we see God's people calling upon Yahweh by His name.

- Moses praised and called upon God by His sacred personal name.

  - Then it came about when the ark set out that Moses said, "Rise up, O Lord [Yahweh]! And let Your enemies be scattered, and let those who hate You flee before You."
    —Numbers 10:35

- Joshua spoke to God using His name, Yahweh.

  - Then Joshua spoke to the Lord [Yahweh] in the day when the Lord [Yahweh] delivered up the Amorites before the sons of Israel.
    —Joshua 10:12

- After Joshua's death, the children of Israel continued calling upon God using His name, Yahweh.

  - Now it came about after the death of Joshua that the sons of Israel inquired of the Lord [Yahweh].
    —Judges 1:1

- Boaz blessed his workers in the field using God's name, Yahweh, and the workers in return blessed Boaz in the name of Yahweh.

  - Now behold, Boaz came from Bethlehem and said to the reapers, "May the LORD [Yahweh] be with you." And they said to him, "May the LORD [Yahweh] bless you."

    —RUTH 2:4

- Hannah made a vow to God using His name, Yahweh.

  - She made a vow and said, "O LORD [Yahweh] of hosts, if You will indeed look on the affliction of Your maidservant and remember me, and not forget Your maidservant, but will give Your maidservant a son, then I will give him to the LORD [Yahweh] all the days of his life, and a razor shall never come on his head."

    —1 SAMUEL 1:11

- David proclaimed that Yahweh would deliver him from the Philistines, and King Saul blessed David in the name of Yahweh.

  - And David said, "The LORD [Yahweh] who delivered me from the paw of the lion and from the paw of the bear, He will deliver me from the hand of this Philistine." And Saul said to David, "Go, and may the LORD [Yahweh] be with you."

    —1 SAMUEL 17:37

From the time of Moses, the entire Hebrew nation called upon God not simply as Lord but by His sacred personal name, Yahweh. It was Yahweh's desire for Israel to know

His name and to call upon Him using it, and this is still His desire for us today when done lovingly and in the holy fear of God.

One difficulty we have in calling upon God's name, however, is that we cannot be absolutely sure of its proper pronunciation. When the Temple in Jerusalem was destroyed in AD 70 and the priesthood scattered, the Jewish people stopped using the name Yahweh altogether, and its pronunciation was eventually lost.

Because the ancient Hebrew language contained only twenty-two consonants and no vowels, the only way you knew how to pronounce a word was by hearing it, and pronunciation of words was passed down verbally from generation to generation.

Today, Hebrew words have vowel markings along with the consonants to help us know how to pronounce the word. However, in the ancient world there were no vowel markings. Those weren't added until sometime between the seventh and tenth centuries.

This is partly why many in the Gentile church pronounce God's personal name as Jehovah instead of Yahweh. To keep Gentile nations from using Father God's name to mock or blaspheme Him, the ancient Jewish scribes deliberately placed the vowel markings incorrectly. Another factor is that what was originally a *y* sound in ancient Hebrew was eventually translated from Hebrew to Greek as an *I* and in some cases from Greek to Latin as a *J*. This is how *Yisrael* became *Israel* and *Yerushalayim* transformed into *Jerusalem*.

Because we don't have the vowel markings for Yahweh's name, and because God's sacred covenant name stopped being spoken so that the oral transmission of its pronunciation was broken and lost, we can't be 100 percent sure how to pronounce it. Yet despite those challenges, most Semitic scholars who have studied the ancient Hebrew language believe the letters *yod*, *hey*, *vav*, *hey*, which compose the name YWWH, are pronounced as a breathy "Yahweh."

Experience More of Him!

God revealed His personal name to us to show us who He is, that He loves us, and that He desires to have an intimate, personal relationship with us—not just in heaven but here on earth right now.

You will experience closeness with Father God when you put Him first in your life and seek Him with all your heart. When you do this, He will manifest His presence to you in a greater way. The Lord will speak to you, and He will walk with you and guide you through your life. In Jeremiah 29:13–14 He said this: "'You will seek Me and find Me when you search for Me with all your heart. I will be found by you,' declares the Lord [Yahweh]."

If you desire to experience God in these ways, then you must consecrate yourself unto Him. In order for Moses to come into the Lord's presence at the burning bush, he first needed to consecrate himself by removing his dirty sandals because he was on holy ground (Exod. 3:4–5).

Before the Israelites could come into the presence of God, they also needed to consecrate themselves.

> The Lord also said to Moses, "Go to the people and consecrate them today and tomorrow, and let them wash their garments; and let them be ready for the third

day, for on the third day the LORD will come down on
Mount Sinai in the sight of all the people."

—EXODUS 19:10–11

Just as Moses and the Israelites needed to consecrate
themselves before God would manifest His presence to
them, you too must consecrate yourself in order to experience more of God's presence in your life. You need to be
cleansed of all the things in your life that are self-serving
and self-seeking and instead come under His authority in
obedience.

Instead of gossiping, laughing at inappropriate jokes,
and otherwise indulging your flesh, seize hold of Yahweh,
making Him yours, here and now. Apprehend Him by faith,
not as a God who is far away but one who is here for you
right now.

He's the blessing, the prize, and the reward!

CHAPTER 6

YAHWEH YIREH—THE LORD OUR PROVIDER

MANY TIMES IN Scripture, God uses His personal name, Yahweh, in conjunction with a saving activity He performs in the lives of those who are in covenant relationship with Him. In the next several chapters we are going to look at eight of these covenant names. It is my prayer that seeing how God combines His personal name with what He does for His children will embolden us to trust Him to do those things for us.

You see, there are certain things we can hope God will do. We can hope He will give us a particular job, for instance, or bless us with a spouse or children. But there are things we can be sure of and know that He will do. The things we can most definitely trust Him for are the promises He has made to us in relation to the names through which He has entered into a covenant relationship with us. There's a banner over us, beloved, and that banner is Father God's name. He has covered our lives by His name, and in His name He supplies everything we will ever need.

Nowhere is that clearer than in God's covenant name Yahweh Yireh, which means "the Lord Will Provide" (Gen. 22:14). *Yireh* comes from the Hebrew word *ra'â*, which means "to see." So when we say Yahweh Yireh, we're actually saying God is the One who sees. He sees our needs and provides for them.

You may be familiar with this name but have heard it pronounced Jehovah Jireh rather than Yahweh Yireh. As I mentioned in the previous chapter, this is because those translating the Hebrew Scriptures mistakenly changed the *y* sound in Yahweh Yireh to a *j* sound, thus changing *Yahweh Yireh* to "Jehovah Jireh." This is also how *Yerushalayim* came to be pronounced "Jerusalem" and *Yudah* became "Judah."

There are many well-known Christian songs that speak of Jehovah Jireh, and I've enjoyed them as much as anyone else. I don't share this information for anyone to use it pridefully or to put down those who don't have this knowledge. I am simply clarifying that the correct Hebrew for the covenant name that means "the Lord Sees and Will Provide" is not *Jehovah Jireh* but *Yahweh Yireh*.

Abraham's Encounter With Yahweh Yireh

Father God reveals Himself as Yahweh Yireh in Genesis 22, where He calls Abraham to sacrifice his son Isaac as a burnt offering on a mountain in the land of Moriah.

> Now it came about after these things, that God tested Abraham, and said to him, "Abraham!" And he said, "Here I am." He said, "Take now your son, your only son, whom you love, Isaac, and go to the land of Moriah, and offer him there as a burnt offering on one of the mountains of which I will tell you." So Abraham rose early in

the morning and saddled his donkey, and took two of his young men with him and Isaac his son; and he split wood for the burnt offering, and arose and went to the place of which God had told him.

—GENESIS 22:1–3

On the third day of Abraham and Isaac's journey to the mountain, Isaac asks his father where the lamb is for the burnt offering, and Abraham tells Isaac that God Himself will provide the sacrifice. Then, after reaching the mountain where he is to sacrifice his son, Abraham builds an altar and lays Isaac upon it. In complete obedience to God, Abraham takes a knife to slay his son, and just as Abraham is about to kill Isaac, the Lord stops him.

But the angel of the LORD called to him from heaven and said, "Abraham, Abraham!" And he said, "Here I am." He said, "Do not stretch out your hand against the lad, and do nothing to him; for now I know that you fear God, since you have not withheld your son, your only son, from Me." Then Abraham raised his eyes and looked, and behold, behind him a ram caught in the thicket by his horns; and Abraham went and took the ram and offered him up for a burnt offering in the place of his son.

—GENESIS 22:11–13

The Scriptures go on to say, "Abraham called the name of that place The LORD Will Provide [Yahweh Yireh], as it is said to this day, 'In the mount of the LORD it will be provided'" (Gen. 22:14). This historical place where God revealed Himself to Abraham as Yahweh Yireh is located in Jerusalem and is the site where the first and second Temples stood, both Solomon's Temple and the one that existed during Yeshua's earthly ministry.

Currently, the Muslim Dome of the Rock sits at this location, and because of this, some have suggested that when the Temple is rebuilt in fulfillment of end-time prophecy (Ezek. 37:28), it will be erected at another site. But according to Jewish tradition, the Temple can be built only on Mount Moriah in the place where Abraham went to sacrifice Isaac.

The binding of Isaac, or the *Akedah* as it's called in Hebrew, remains an important moment for more reasons than its location. It also holds incredible prophetic significance.

Many of the pictures we see of Abraham binding Isaac on Mount Moriah present Isaac as a young child, but according to Jewish tradition, he was around thirty-seven years old. This tells us Isaac wasn't a passive observer in this incredible act of obedience; he was a willing participant.

When we consider that Isaac freely yielded his life to his father in complete trust, we see an image of Messiah Jesus Himself foreshadowed in him. Like Isaac, an adult who willingly offered up his life in obedience to his father, Abraham, so too does Yeshua willingly offer up His own life in obedience to Father God. While no sacrifice would be comparable to the one Jesus made when He gave Himself up for the sin of the world, Isaac, like Yeshua, knowingly and fully offered up his own life on that altar.

This is not the only way the Akedah was fulfilled in Yeshua. Jewish thought teaches that this act opened up a channel for God's grace to be released upon Israel and the whole world. The rabbinic teaching is that before the binding of Isaac, God's grace was largely shut off from the earth, but Abraham's act of obedience and Isaac's act of radical surrender opened up a channel for the grace of God to come upon the nation of Israel, and through Israel to flood the entire world. The faithful sacrifice of the one (Isaac) opened floodgates of mercy for the many.

So too when Messiah Jesus, the Lamb of God, gave up His life and paid the price for the sin of mankind, He opened a channel of blessing to the whole world. As John 3:16 says, "For God so loved the world, that He gave His only begotten Son, that whoever believes in Him shall not perish, but have eternal life."

Through the covenant we have with God through our faith in Yeshua, we can be assured that He will meet *all* our needs, whether they are physical, emotional, relational, or spiritual. Yahweh Yireh is not only the One who provided for Abraham and the Jewish people; He will provide for every single child of His—to this day.

Yeshua said, "Do not worry then, saying, 'What will we eat?' or 'What will we drink?' or 'What will we wear for clothing?' For the Gentiles eagerly seek all these things; for your heavenly Father knows that you need all these things" (Matt. 6:31–32). If Father God provides for the lilies of the field and the birds of the air, as Matthew 6 says, will He not take care of His own children? This does not mean He will give us everything we could ever want, but we can count on Him to sustain us and meet our true needs. Beloved, people who don't know God should worry about what they'll eat and wear, but not you and I, because our God is Yahweh Yireh.

Will You Pass the Test?

People often wonder why God tested Abraham by calling him to sacrifice Isaac. Was He not sure whether Abraham would pass or fail?

When we think of tests, we often envision the ones taken in school. The teacher presents the material, and then the students are tested to prove to both the teacher and the students that the material has been learned. It's different with God. When He tests us, it's not to see whether we'll pass or fail. He already knows what we're going to do. By putting us to the test, God helps us discover what's within us. His test is designed to bring us to a higher, more perfect level of obedience to Him.

God already knew Abraham's heart, and by putting him to the test, He was perfecting Abraham in his obedience. The Lord never intended for Abraham to sacrifice his son; He knew all along that He would provide a ram for the sacrifice, a substitute for Isaac. So too God tests you, not to see if you'll pass or fail. He tests you because He loves you and through the test is transforming you; moving you forward to a higher, more perfect level of obedience to Him; and further conforming you into the image of His Son.

When God told Abraham to sacrifice his only son, Abraham was being required to give up the thing in his life that he loved the most. And because Abraham gave it up, God blessed him in a way that was far beyond anything Abraham could ever have dreamed. The Lord told him:

> Because you have done this thing and have not withheld your son, your only son, indeed I will greatly bless you, and I will greatly multiply your seed as the stars of the heavens and as the sand which is on the seashore; and your seed shall possess the gate of their enemies. In your seed all the nations of the earth shall be blessed, because you have obeyed My voice.
>
> —Genesis 22:16–18

Abraham was greatly blessed because of his perfect obedi-ence to God, and Yahweh Yireh will bless our obedience too. Yeshua said if we seek first God's kingdom and His righ-teousness, "all these things will be added" to us (Matt. 6:33).

In this account we also see the great faith of Abraham. He told his servants, "Stay here with the donkey, and I and the lad will go over there; and *we will worship and return to you*" (Gen. 22:5). He believed both he and Isaac would be returning. We read in the Book of Hebrews:

> By faith Abraham…offered up Isaac….He considered that God is able to raise people even from the dead, from which he also received him back as a type.
> —Hebrews 11:17, 19

Because of his faith, Abraham not only became the father of the nation of Israel; he became the father of all who would come to faith in Yeshua (Rom. 4:16; Gal. 3:6). And because of his extravagant obedience, God blessed him to live to the ripe old age of 175, and Abraham died "an old man and satisfied with life" (Gen. 25:8).

If we are willing to be obedient and go all the way with God, Yahweh will extravagantly bless us too, just as He did Abraham. Yahweh Yireh sees our every need, and in His love He will abundantly provide for us. The apostle Paul said, "And my God will supply all your needs according to His riches in glory in [Messiah] Jesus" (Phil. 4:19).

God does not promise to satisfy all our desires, but He will provide everything we truly need. David said, "I have been young and now I am old, yet I have not seen the righ-teous forsaken or his descendants begging bread" (Ps. 37:25). We can be certain Father God will supply all our true needs according to His riches in glory. Beloved, you'll always have food in your stomach. You'll always have a roof over your head. God is going to take care of His children, and He wants us to believe He will do that. He provides for every single one of His children who are in a covenant relationship with Him. He is Yahweh Yireh.

I know sometimes it's hard to believe God will provide when we find ourselves in difficult places in life. But I want to issue a challenge, beloved. When we have a need and we're battling fear and doubt, let's declare, "Father, You are Yahweh Yireh to me; You will provide." God is the same yesterday, today, and forever, and He will always be your Yahweh Yireh, your Lord who sees and will provide for you.

CHAPTER 7

YAHWEH ROPHEKA—THE LORD OUR HEALER

Most Americans believe in supernatural healing. A 2016 Barna Group study found that roughly two-thirds of respondents (66 percent) believe in miraculous healing, about the same percentage (68 percent) have prayed for someone to be healed, and just over a quarter (27 percent) have actually experienced divine healing.[1] Yet this is an area where believers often struggle in their faith, especially if they prayed for healing and did not experience a restoration of their health. But as we will see in this chapter, we don't have to question whether our God heals. We can seek Him for health and healing because He has revealed Himself as Yahweh Ropheka, "the Lord our Healer."

Father God demonstrates His power to heal throughout the Hebrew Bible. He healed Hannah of infertility (1 Sam. 1:20), Naaman of leprosy (2 Kings 5:14), and Hezekiah of a life-threatening illness (2 Kings 20:7)—and that just scratches the surface. He also brought two widows' sons back to life (1 Kings 17:17–22; 2 Kings 4:32–35), and He used the prophet

Elisha's bones to raise a man from the dead (2 Kings 13:21). God is clearly a healer, and He reveals Himself as one by name in Exodus 15, where our Lord makes Himself known as Yahweh Ropheka.

In this chapter, the Lord has parted the Red Sea, allowing the Israelites to escape the Egyptians, and the Israelites had been traveling in the wilderness for three days with no water in sight. When they reached a place called Marah, they found water, but it was too bitter to drink. In fact, drinking it would have made the people sick.

So Moses cried out to God for help, and the Lord commanded Moses to place a certain tree into the water. When Moses did, God made the unhealthy, bitter water sweet, and the people were able to drink it. Then He said:

> If you will give earnest heed to the voice of the LORD your God, and do what is right in His sight, and give ear to His commandments, and keep all His statutes, I will put none of the diseases on you which I have put on the Egyptians; for I, the LORD [Yahweh], am your healer [Rophe or Ropheka].
>
> —Exodus 15:26

Father God brought the Israelites to a place of testing and barrenness in order to make Himself known as their healer, and He wants us to trust Him for healing as well. God is not just the One who brought healing to the ancient Israelites; He is our healer today. We too can experience Him as the Lord who heals because Messiah Yeshua bore our sin and sickness in His body on the cross. Father God, by nature and character, is a healer.

In his beautiful and dynamic Messianic prophecy, Isaiah

declared, "But He was pierced through for our transgressions, He was crushed for our iniquities; the chastening for our well-being fell upon Him, and by His scourging we are healed" (Isa. 53:5; see also Matthew 8:17). When Messiah Jesus died on the cross, He not only paid the price to redeem us from our sins; He also made provision for our healing. The blessing of Yahweh Ropheka is imparted to us through Messiah Yeshua, and by His wounds we are healed.

It may be hard to reconcile this when we've prayed for healing and our condition doesn't change. This happened to me several years ago, and it led to an intense crisis of faith. I had suffered from acid reflux for many years and had been prescribed medication, but over time the medicine began irritating my throat and making my voice hoarse. I was concerned the medication would eventually damage my vocal cords, which would be devastating for me as a preacher. So I decided to trust Yahweh Ropheka as my healer and stop taking the medication. I stood on healing scriptures, but after months of waiting on the Lord, my condition didn't improve.

I was devastated. I didn't understand why God didn't respond to my faith by healing me. I was so hurt I began to wonder if I could even trust God for salvation since it seemed I couldn't trust Him to heal me.

In time, the Lord started bringing various passages of Scripture to my attention. He reminded me that Paul suffered from a thorn in his flesh that was never taken away (2 Cor. 12:7–10). Paul also left his traveling companion Trophimus sick at Miletus, and he encouraged his protégé Timothy to drink a little wine for his stomach problems and frequent ailments (2 Tim. 4:20; 1 Tim. 5:23).

I came to understand there is an element of mystery to divine healing. Isaiah 53:5 says by our Lord's stripes we are healed—present tense—so we all will experience supernatural healing. But some will be healed immediately, while others will be healed over time, and some won't experience healing until they are with Father God and Yeshua in heaven. Even though we can't explain why it seems some people get healed and others don't, let's not allow what we don't understand to keep us from taking hold of what we do know to be true.

The Word of God tells us clearly that Yahweh is a God who heals. In fact, everywhere Messiah Jesus went, He did three things: He preached the gospel, healed the sick, and delivered those who were oppressed by demons. When He sent His disciples out two by two to minister, He told them to do the same three things, saying: "And as you go, preach, saying, 'The kingdom of heaven is at hand.' Heal the sick, raise the dead, cleanse the lepers, cast out demons. Freely you received, freely give" (Matt. 10:7–9).

God's Word is consistent and true. Father God is the healer of His people. We can trust Him to be Yahweh Ropheka, even if our healing does not come exactly when we want it to. And there are principles we can glean from Scripture to more fully understand the mystery and balance of divine healing.

Experiencing Yahweh as Our Healer

First, notice that in Exodus 15:26, God didn't simply promise to be our healer. He said, "*If* you will give earnest heed to the voice of the LORD your God, and do what is right in His sight, and give ear to His commandments, and keep all His statutes, I will put none of the diseases on you which I have put on the Egyptians." The Lord was telling the children of Israel that in order to experience Him as their healer, they had to walk in His ways. They had to be listening for His voice and yielding to His Word, His will, and His Spirit.

Why do I point this out? Many Christians today want to be healed, yet they live irresponsibly and practice unhealthy habits. They don't exercise; they overeat; they don't monitor their cholesterol; they consume too much sugar—the list goes on. Beloved, it's not enough to expect Father God to be our healer. We also have to cooperate with Him. Our bodies are the temple of the Holy Spirit, and we must be conscious of that when we're choosing how to live. We can trust God to be our healer, but we have a part to play.

I don't say that to condemn anyone. If you've done your best to live for God and yet you're still struggling with an illness, I make no judgment at all. I don't know why some get healed instantly, some get healed over a period of time, and some don't experience their complete healing until they meet God face to face. What I know is that God is your healer and you're going to know perfect healing in your life, whether now or later. Again, let's not allow what we don't understand to keep us from taking hold of the truth we do understand.

Yahweh Is Sovereign

I want to make another observation about Exodus 15:26 that many believers have a hard time accepting. The verse says, "If you will give earnest heed to the voice of the LORD your God...*I will put none of the diseases on you which I have put on the Egyptians.*"

Many people teach that sickness is never of God. But who put the diseases on the Egyptians in Exodus 15:26? God did, and we see elsewhere in Scripture where He takes responsibility for putting illness on people.

For example, when the Israelites were in the wilderness grumbling against God, He sent serpents to bite them, and many people died (Num. 21). And in the Book of Deuteronomy, the Lord said He would bring diseases on the Israelites if they disobeyed the Law:

> If you are not careful to observe all the words of this law which are written in this book, to fear this honored and awesome name, the LORD your God, then *the* LORD *will bring extraordinary plagues on you and your descendants*, even severe and lasting plagues, and miserable and chronic sicknesses. He will bring back on you all the diseases of Egypt of which you were afraid, and they will cling to you.
>
> —DEUTERONOMY 28:58–60

We see this also in the New Testament. In the Book of Revelation, God said concerning Jezebel: "I gave her time to repent, and she does not want to repent of her immorality. Behold, *I will throw her on a bed of sickness*, and those who commit adultery with her into great tribulation, unless they repent of her deeds" (Rev. 2:21–22). Those who say God never puts sickness on people are putting blinders on their eyes, because there are clear examples in the Bible where God uses sickness to accomplish His objectives.

God is never interested in keeping a person permanently sick. That is completely outside His nature. But to say He never uses sickness is to deny the Word of God, because it's evident that at times He does. Father God is good, and in Him there is no darkness at all. But as I said in a previous chapter, He is Adon Olam—the Master of the universe—and He uses all things, including sickness, to accomplish His purpose.

Please don't misunderstand. It is God's will that we walk in divine health. Yeshua taught us to pray, "Your kingdom come. Your will be done, on earth as it is in heaven" (Matt. 6:10), and in heaven there is no sickness. God desires for us to be healthy. But sometimes there's a difference between the eternal will of God and the temporal will of God. On occasion God will allow or cause sickness to come upon His people as a consequence of sin. Sometimes He uses sickness to demonstrate His power in a person's life. And at times He allows or causes sickness because He knows it will bring the person to a place of dependence on Him.

This is what Paul speaks of in 2 Corinthians 12:7–10:

> To keep me from exalting myself, there was given me a thorn in the flesh, a messenger of Satan to torment me—to keep me from exalting myself! Concerning this I implored the Lord three times that it might leave me. And He has said to me, "My grace is sufficient for you, for power is perfected in weakness." Most gladly, therefore, I will rather boast about my weaknesses, so that the power of Christ may dwell in me. Therefore I am well content with weaknesses, with insults, with distresses, with persecutions, with difficulties, for Christ's sake; for when I am weak, then I am strong.

We don't know for sure what the thorn in his flesh was. It could have been someone who was persecuting Paul; we just don't know. But the principle is the same. The thorn in Paul's flesh was a messenger of Satan, and God orchestrated and used it.

In fact, Paul himself said that because of the abundance of the revelation he had been given, God sent the thorn in his flesh "to keep me from exalting myself!" He recognized that the thorn in his flesh was by God's design to keep him clinging to Jesus and help him avoid becoming prideful. This messenger of Satan was actually a gift to Paul, not only because it kept him on his knees but also because it made him weak, and in his weakness, God's power was built in his life.

My point is that God is a healer. His ultimate purpose is that His people will walk continually in divine, supernatural, effervescent health. But we must understand that there is a difference between the temporal and the eternal, and sometimes we must pass through hardship in the temporal because God has a purpose in the difficulties. God sometimes uses evil to accomplish a higher good.

Even Adam and Eve's fall in the Garden of Eden brought about God's purposes. Adam and Eve were walking with God in the garden. They knew Him. Then Satan came in and deceived them. Did God want Adam and Eve to fall? Some would say no, but I believe the answer is yes.

I say that because if Adam hadn't fallen, Jesus would never have been glorified as the Savior of the world. When we meet Yeshua face to face, we're going to throw our crowns at His feet and worship Him forever as our Savior and Redeemer. If Adam and Eve had never fallen, Jesus would not have been honored and glorified through human beings the same way.

And consider this: the Bible tells us the first Adam, who was in the Garden of Eden, was a living soul, but the second Adam, Messiah Jesus, is a life-giving Spirit. The first Adam lived in God's presence, but the second Adam, Yeshua, has given us His own Spirit, so the church is actually born of

His Spirit. This is why Jesus said, "Truly, truly, I say to you, unless one is born of water and the Spirit he cannot enter into the kingdom of God. That which is born of the flesh is flesh, and that which is born of the Spirit is spirit. Do not be amazed that I said to you, 'You must be born again'" (John 3:5–7).

The first Adam wasn't born again. He lived in God's presence, but he wasn't born internally of God's Spirit. After Adam fell, you and I—those of us who have been redeemed through Jesus—were given the gift of God's own Spirit to live inside us. We actually are at a much higher place than the first Adam ever was because God's nature is now part of our own.

We cannot fully know the mind of the Lord. He works all things after the counsel of His own will and causes all things to work together for good for those who love Him and are called according to His purposes (Eph. 1:11; Rom. 8:28). The Lord says, "For My thoughts are not your thoughts, nor are your ways My ways...For as the heavens are higher than the earth, so are My ways higher than your ways and My thoughts than your thoughts" (Isa. 55:8–9).

While we cannot understand the Lord, we can be confident that His banner over us is healing and God's will is for us to walk in health. But we need to be humble and rely on Him in order to receive that blessing. If we're not, He may send sickness to get us to that place of humility. The Lord disciplines everyone whom He receives (Heb. 12:6), and sometimes He may use sickness to do that. This is what happened when Aaron and Miriam began to blaspheme Moses in Numbers 12. God struck Miriam with leprosy, bringing correction to her and Aaron.

Trust God, Not Man, to Heal

That brings me to a third observation I want to make about the account in Exodus 15:26. Father God said, "I, the LORD, am your healer." Beloved, we must remember that the Lord is the source of our health and healing.

In 2 Chronicles 16 we read that King Asa developed a severe disease in his feet. But instead of seeking the Lord, he sought the physicians:

> In the thirty-ninth year of his reign Asa became dis-eased in his feet. His disease was severe, yet even in his disease he did not seek the LORD, but the physicians. So Asa slept with his fathers, having died in the forty-first year of his reign.
> —2 CHRONICLES 16:12–13

The implication is that Asa would have lived had he sought Yahweh Ropheka instead of trusting only in the physicians.

We live in a world that is so scientifically advanced that we often rely on modern medicine to sustain us. We start to feel sick, and we turn to the doctor for a prescription to treat what ails us. Without question, God uses medical professionals, but too often we rely only on science when we are sick instead of seeking the true source of health and healing, Yahweh Ropheka.

As I pointed out earlier, when Moses and the people of Israel came to the bitter waters of Marah, God told Moses to put a tree branch in the water. When he did, the bitter water became sweet, and the Israelites were able to drink it. I believe that tree branch can be compared to medical science today. God sometimes uses medical science to bring healing, even as He used that tree branch to bring health to those bitter waters. But Moses wasn't relying on the tree branch; he was relying on Yahweh Ropheka. Beloved, we should always be looking to the Lord for healing, even when we go to doctors. Instead of putting our confidence in physicians as Asa did, we must trust the Lord as our healer.

Several years ago, I had an experience in which Father God clearly revealed Himself to me as Yahweh Ropheka, the Lord my healer. I was preparing to minster in Gulu, Uganda, and was set to leave on a Monday. But the Friday before I was to depart, I started noticing that my blood pressure was getting really high, and I had pain in my heart that wasn't going away. To make the situation more complicated, I was traveling that day to minister in Toledo, Ohio, over the weekend. Then I was to go straight to Detroit to fly out to Gulu on Monday.

As the day progressed that Friday, I started to get really concerned. I knew the hospitals in Gulu weren't as sophisticated as the ones in my city, so I decided to go to the doctor to get checked out before traveling to Toledo. They performed an EKG and took some tests; then I went home. A couple hours later, the doctor called and said the EKG results weren't normal and she wanted me to go in for another EKG. I told her I was packing for my trip to Toledo and then I would be going on to Uganda, so I didn't have time to get the test. She was concerned by my response and said, "You need to take your health seriously."

I had been preaching to my congregation that God is our healer, and I told them we can't fear negative reports from doctors; we have to trust God. As I said, I believe God uses doctors, but I wanted to challenge myself with the truth I had been preaching. I wanted to believe God to be my healer. So I said, "God, I'm going to trust You in this," and I went to Toledo.

In Toledo, my blood pressure was still high, my heart still hurt, and I was starting to get really concerned. As I was lying in bed that weekend, I started thinking it would be irresponsible for me to go to Gulu with what was going on. The doctor told me something wasn't right, and I was still experiencing pain in my chest and couldn't get my blood pressure down. So I told the Lord, "I really want to believe You to be my healer, but my wife needs me; my children need me."

As I was wrestling with this in the middle of the night, my wife, Cynthia, woke up, and I told her I didn't think I should go to Gulu. To my surprise, faith rose up in Cynthia, and she began to declare over me that many people were going to get saved and lives were going to be changed when I ministered in Gulu. I was surprised by her response because Cynthia is very protective of me. It was truly the inspiration and boldness of God that rose up in her. I knew her prayer was coming from God because it was so unlike my wife to be praying for me like that and telling me I should go to Uganda when I was in a potentially dangerous situation in the natural. I went back to sleep.

When I woke up the next morning, I again had fear. I knew I needed to hear from the Lord, so I asked Him to confirm whether He wanted me to go to Gulu. I was in the midst of doing my devotional that morning, so I had my Bible in my hands, and I said, "Lord, I really need to hear from You. If You want me to go to Gulu, Father, please speak to me." Then I opened the Bible, not knowing where it would open because this was a brand-new Bible, and when I looked down, my eyes landed on Exodus 15:26, the only verse in the entire Word of God where the Lord reveals Himself as Yahweh Ropheka, the Lord our Healer.

> And He said, "If you will give earnest heed to the voice of the LORD your God, and do what is right in His sight, and give ear to His commandments, and keep all His statutes, I will put none of the diseases on you which I have put on the Egyptians; for I, the LORD, am your healer."
>
> —EXODUS 15:26

When that happened, my heart was pierced as if with a sword, and I began to weep. My weeping was twofold: I was so thankful to have been touched by Father God so forcefully. But I was also weeping in repentance because I was deeply convicted that some of the pain I was feeling in my heart was a result of stress I had allowed into my life. In Exodus 15:26, God says that to experience His healing salvation as my reality, I have to "give earnest heed" to His voice. I realized I had not been fully trusting Him with the details of my life and was stressed as a result. I promised the Lord I would no longer allow toxic thoughts to invade my mind and create stress but would instead rest in Him.

I took authority over that pain in my heart and was completely healed. I went to Gulu and saw an incredible move of God, and the pain did not return, because Father God is Yahweh Ropheka. He is the Lord our Healer, and He is faithful.

Some people think trusting in God means we should not seek help from modern medicine. But as I pointed out in my book *Experiencing the Supernatural*, I think there is a balance to strike. Paul referred to Luke as "the beloved physician" in Colossians 4:14, and I see no reason to believe Luke had stopped practicing medicine at the time of Paul's writing. While I absolutely believe in seeking God for divine healing, I do not think we should reject the assistance of medical professionals after first turning to Yahweh Ropheka. In my opinion, God can heal in various ways, sometimes through miraculous means and at other times through medical intervention.

The Lord may choose to use natural remedies such as herbs or prescription medications, or He may work through physicians to bring about healing. As the ultimate authority, God heals in the way He deems best, which may at times be unknown to us. For example, when I was struggling with a medical issue several years ago, the Lord showed me in a dream to use a combination of herbs, including one I had never heard of before. I obeyed, and I was healed.

We can learn from the story of Naaman, the captain of King Aram's army, who had contracted leprosy. (See 1 Kings 5:1–14.) The king sent Naaman to the prophet Elisha in Israel to be healed. Naaman expected Elisha to heal him in a spectacular manner, but instead Elisha instructed Naaman to wash in the Jordan River seven times. To make matters worse, Elisha did not even talk to Naaman personally; he sent his messenger. Though initially frustrated, Naaman followed Elisha's instructions at the urging of his servants, and he was ultimately healed.

I would prefer to never use modern medicine. But I have found that sometimes the Lord heals me supernaturally, and sometimes He chooses to use medicine or physicians. It is important that we maintain a balanced approach. We must always be looking to the Lord as the ultimate source of healing while remaining open to the methods He chooses to use.[2]

The Spirit Gives Us Life

We can trust God to sustain our health and give life to our flesh so we can be healthy even when we're old. In other words, Father God gives life to our mortal bodies through His indwelling Spirit. The apostle Paul speaks to this:

> But if the Spirit of Him who raised Jesus from the dead dwells in you, He who raised Christ Jesus from the dead will also give life to your mortal bodies through His Spirit who dwells in you.
>
> —ROMANS 8:11

The Spirit of God Himself within us is giving life to our flesh. "Though our outer man is decaying," Paul wrote, "yet our inner man is being renewed day by day" (2 Cor. 4:16). God's Spirit within us is ministering life to our flesh to keep us healthy. Yes, we're still going to age and our natural bodies are going to degenerate, but we can be healthy even when we're old because the healer is in us and He is sustaining us. God's Word says, "The law of the Spirit of life in Christ Jesus has set you free from the law of sin and of death" (Rom. 8:2).

Abraham lived to the ripe old age of 175, and he was healthy and satisfied with his life when he died (Gen. 25:7–8). The Bible says when Moses died at 120, he had not lost his vigor. He still had a spirit of youth and healthfulness because the blessing of the Lord was upon him (Deut. 34:7).

The same is available to you and me. God's blessings are imparted to us through the Spirit of Messiah who lives inside us. We have the health of Yahweh Ropheka because

Messiah Jesus bore our sin and sickness in His body on the cross, and by His wounds we are healed.

When Yeshua walked the earth, He went about "healing every kind of disease and every kind of sickness among the people" (Matt. 4:23). He is the same yesterday, today, and forever. No matter what sickness you may face, it's not too big for Yeshua to heal. Messiah Jesus is the name above every name, and "at the name of Jesus every knee will bow, of those who are in heaven and on earth and under the earth, and...every tongue will confess that Jesus Christ is Lord, to the glory of God the Father" (Phil. 2:10–11). Every demon in hell and every sickness on this earth is subject to His name.

Yahweh Heals the Brokenhearted

The Lord heals not only our physical sickness and disease; He also heals broken hearts. As He began His ministry, one of the first things Yeshua did was go into the Temple on the Sabbath and read from the scroll of Isaiah, proclaiming:

> "The Spirit of the Lord is upon Me, because He has anointed Me to preach the gospel to the poor; *He has sent Me to heal the broken-hearted*, to preach deliverance to the captives and recovery of sight to the blind, to set at liberty those who are oppressed; to preach the acceptable year of the Lord." Then He rolled up the scroll, and He gave it back to the attendant, and sat down. The eyes of all those who were in the synagogue were fixed on Him. And He began to say to them, "Today this Scripture is fulfilled in your hearing."
>
> —Luke 4:18–21, mev

We hear a lot about the Lord being the healer of our physical sickness, but we don't hear enough about Him being the healer of our broken hearts. The psalmist sang of how Yeshua would gather unto Himself those who were hurting and heal their brokenness.

> The LORD builds up Jerusalem; He gathers the outcasts of Israel. He heals the brokenhearted and binds up their wounds.
>
> —PSALM 147:2–3

Sometimes things happen to us in life that are so shattering time will not heal those wounds. Only the Lord can heal them. Some have been left broken by divorce. Others are hurt over abuse, rejection, the loss of a loved one, or the rebellion of a wayward child. Whatever has left you brokenhearted, Yahweh Ropheka is the healer. He has come in the person of Yeshua to heal you physically and emotionally, so cry out and cling to Him.

The Lord causes all things to work together for good in our lives, and sometimes He allows us to experience these broken places so we come to depend on Him. You may remember in Genesis 32 when God changed Jacob's name to Israel. Jacob came to a place he would later call Peniel, where he wrestled with God all night. Even though he must have been exhausted, Jacob refused to give up. He told the Lord, "I will not let you go unless you bless me" (Gen. 32:26).

Jacob left that wrestling match forever changed. First, he left with a new name. Jacob means "supplanter,"[3] and that's who Jacob had been his whole life. He was born with his hand on his twin brother's heel, and he eventually stole his brother Esau's birthright. But that day, God changed his name to Israel, which means one who struggles with God.

Jacob also left Peniel with a limp he carried for the rest

of his life. I believe prophetically that limp symbolizes that place of being broken before the Lord. Jacob's limp was a constant reminder that when he was broken before God and began to cling to the Lord and say, "I'm never going to let go of You," God changed his life.

In a similar way, sometimes the Lord will use the very thing that caused us so much pain to transform us and bring wholeness and blessing into our lives. Yahweh Ropheka wants us to prosper and be in good health, even as our soul prospers (3 John 2). He wants to bring us to a place of wholeness and recovery. But He wants us to depend on and cling to Him for our healing.

We must become like Moses when he was leading the Israelites toward the Promised Land. He told Father God, "If Your presence does not go with us, do not lead us up from here" (Exod. 33:15). Moses refused to travel any farther until they had assurance the Lord was with them.

Unfortunately, some of us are too arrogant to come to that place of humility. Rather than saying, "God, I'm not going until I know You are with me," we just run out and do our own thing. We jump out of bed in the morning and rush off to work without even thinking about God. Maybe we think about Him for a second, but for the most part our minds are on other things. When we're sick, we call the doctor and don't turn to God to request His help.

If you desire to live and walk in divine health, you must depend on and cling to the very source of health, Yahweh Ropheka, every minute of every day. When you open your heart and cleave to Him, He will be your source of life and divine health.

CHAPTER 8

YAHWEH NISSI—THE LORD OUR VICTORY BANNER

SHORTLY AFTER YAHWEH made Himself known to the children of Israel as their healer, He revealed Himself as Yahweh Nissi, which means "the Lord our Banner," or "the Lord our Victory." As is the case with all the revelations of His name, the Master of the universe disclosed this aspect of His divine nature in response to a need of His people that couldn't be met in the natural.

Soon after Moses led the Israelites out of Egypt, they were suddenly attacked by a fearsome people called the Amalekites. These were descendants of Amalek, the grandson of Jacob's twin brother, Esau (Gen. 36:12). Yet despite having common ancestors with the Israelites, the Amalekites seemed to have nothing but animosity for the Jewish people.

Well-trained in warfare, the Amalekites were too numerous and powerful for the Israelites to defeat. Bear in mind, the people of Israel had never fought a war before. They had been enslaved in Egypt for more than four hundred years. They were a ragtag group with absolutely no military training—the opposite of today's highly skilled, technologically advanced Israeli army, which is one of the best in the world. The Israelites knew they couldn't win on their own, so they looked to the Lord.

> Then Amalek came and fought against Israel at Rephidim. So Moses said to Joshua, "Choose men for us and go out, fight against Amalek. Tomorrow I will station myself on the top of the hill with the staff of God in my hand." Joshua did as Moses told him, and fought against Amalek; and Moses, Aaron, and Hur went up to the top of the hill. So it came about when Moses held his hand up, that Israel prevailed, and when he let his hand down, Amalek prevailed. But Moses' hands were heavy. Then they took a stone and put it under him, and he sat on it; and Aaron and Hur supported his hands, one on one side and one on the other. Thus his hands were steady until the sun set. So Joshua overwhelmed Amalek and his people with the edge of the sword.
>
> Then the Lord said to Moses, "Write this in a book as a memorial and recite it to Joshua, that I will utterly blot out the memory of Amalek from under heaven." Moses built an altar and named it *The* Lord *is My Banner* [Yahweh Nissi].
>
> —Exodus 17:8–15

The Israelites were victorious in battle because Yahweh Nissi fought for them. When His people needed supernatural deliverance from their enemy, Yahweh became for them a banner, which is a symbol of victory throughout the Scriptures. This pattern is especially evident in the psalms of David.

> We will sing for joy over your victory, and in the name of our God we will set up our banners....Now I know that the Lord saves His anointed; He will answer him

from His holy heaven with the saving strength of His right hand. Some boast in chariots and some in horses, but we will boast in the name of the LORD, our God.

—PSALM 20:5–7

You have given a banner to those who fear You, that it may be displayed because of the truth. *Selah*. That Your beloved may be delivered, save with Your right hand, and answer us!

—PSALM 60:4–5

God is the same yesterday, today, and forever (Heb. 13:8). He is still Yahweh Nissi, and He wants to give us the victory, just as He did for ancient Israel. But the battles we face are not merely physical. Many times what takes place in the physical realm is actually the result of what's happening in the spiritual realm. This is why the Bible says, "Our struggle is not against flesh and blood, but against the rulers, against the powers, against the world forces of this darkness, against the spiritual forces of wickedness in the heavenly places" (Eph. 6:12).

When Moses had his hands raised during the battle with the Amalekites, something supernatural was taking place. He was being spiritually connected to Yahweh Nissi. Israel surely would have been defeated if they had relied on their own strength, but because they depended on God, He caused them to defeat an enemy that in the natural was much more numerous and powerful than they were.

Human strength is insufficient to win the battles we face. We need supernatural power flowing through us. The Bible says, "'Not by might nor by power, but by My Spirit,' says the LORD of hosts" (Zech. 4:6). We need to be strengthened by the Spirit of Life to see victory.

David understood this. He knew he couldn't defeat Goliath in his own strength; the power to conquer the Philistine giant would come from the Lord.

> Then David said to the Philistine, "You come to me with a sword, a spear, and a javelin, but I come to you in the name of the LORD of hosts, the God of the armies of Israel, whom you have taunted. This day the LORD will deliver you up into my hands, and I will strike you down and remove your head from you. And I will give the dead bodies of the army of the Philistines this day to the birds of the sky and the wild beasts of the earth, that all the earth may know that there is a God in Israel, and that all this assembly may know that the LORD does not deliver by sword or by spear; *for the battle is the LORD's and He will give you into our hands.*"
> —1 Samuel 17:45–47

Just as it was with David, we cannot win the battles we face each day in our own strength. We must trust Father God to be Yahweh Nissi, the Lord who strengthens us in battle and gives us victory over our enemies, both visible and invisible.

Victory Is Ours

After Yahweh Nissi gave Israel the victory over the Amalekites, He instructed them to record the victory in a book as a memorial. We too need to record the victories Yahweh Nissi gives us to serve as a memorial that will encourage and strengthen our faith in Him.

Father God was so disgusted with the Amalekites for attacking the Israelites that He promised to utterly wipe out the memory of their name forever. He told the people of Israel:

Remember what Amalek did to you along the way when you came out from Egypt, how he met you along the way and attacked among you all the stragglers at your rear when you were faint and weary; and he did not fear God. Therefore it shall come about when the LORD your God has given you rest from all your surrounding enemies, in the land which the LORD your God gives you as an inheritance to possess, you shall blot out the memory of Amalek from under heaven; you must not forget.

—DEUTERONOMY 25:17–19

In traditional Judaism, the Amalekites have become the symbol of anti-Semitism, and when someone is anti-Semitic, the person is thought to be the spiritual descendant of the Amalekites, the first anti-Semites recorded in Scripture.

Today the Jewish people have a tradition they celebrate called Purim. The celebration of Purim, which usually takes place in February or March, comes from the events recorded in the Book of Esther. In the account, an anti-Semite by the name of Haman devises a plan to exterminate the Jewish people, but the Lord uses Esther to foil Haman's scheme and deliver His people.

The Jewish people celebrate the feast of Purim every year to commemorate their deliverance from the wicked hands of Haman. The festivities include reading through the Megillah, a scroll of the Book of Esther, and whenever Haman's name is read, a noisemaker called a grager is twirled around, making noise to drown out the sound of Haman's name. This is done because the Lord promised to blot out the memory of the Amalekites, the original anti-Semites, from under heaven (Exod. 17:14, 16).

Just as Yahweh fought to deliver the Jewish people during Esther's day, He fights for His children right now, no matter what battle we come up against. But we must realize that sometimes God tells us to stand still and let Him fight for us, as He did when He parted the Red Sea so the Israelites could cross over on dry ground. Yet at other times He engages us in the battle with Him.

Yahweh Nissi didn't give Israel the victory over the Amalekites independent of their own cooperation; He engaged them in the process of winning the battle. Joshua, Moses, Aaron, Hur, and all the Israelites had to enter the battle, fighting with all their heart, soul, mind, and strength to obtain the victory.

This speaks to us of how battles are won today in the Lord; He will give us victory, but He requires us to fight. When the apostle Paul came to the end of his life, he said, "I have fought the good fight, I have finished the course, I have kept the faith" (2 Tim. 4:7). We must fight for victory and freedom in the Spirit, just as the children of Israel had to fight to enter their Promised Land.

I remember a time in my life when I was really struggling with something, and I cried out to God, saying, "What am I going to do?" He spoke two words to me: hard work. God was telling me, "Kirt, I'm going to give you victory over this, but it's going to take hard work on your part. You're going to have to labor with all your strength, and you will overcome." That's how God works in our lives. He allows us to labor in our circumstances, granting us the strength to overcome them, and in the end we are victorious through Him.

This brings to mind a story I read about a man who was ministering to someone who was possessed by a demon. He commanded the demon to leave the person, but it refused to go. This was very unusual because generally when the man commanded a demon to leave, it would leave. He again said, "Lord, I command this demon to leave," but the demon still refused to go.

The Lord then spoke to this minister, saying, "I told you to command the demon to leave in My name, and the demon will leave." So he declared, "In the name of Jesus, I command you to leave this person immediately." Again the demon refused to leave. The minister repeated this a second and then a third time, but the demon would not leave.

The minister again told the Lord, "I told the demon to leave, but it would not leave." Then the Lord spoke to him in a stern voice and said, "I told you if you command the demon to leave in My name, he will leave!" Then suddenly the sternness of the Lord's voice rose in the minister, and he spoke forth in power and authority, saying, "In the name of Jesus, you wicked, foul spirit, I command you to leave right now!" The demon immediately left the person.

For this deliverance minister to cast out the demon, he needed to arise as a warrior in the power and authority of the Lord, and when he did, the demon immediately left.

Fight to Overcome

Beloved, we are called to overcome, but we must fight. There are things in our lives we can cry out to God to help us with, but until we stand up and fight the battle in the power of Yahweh Nissi, we will never achieve the victory.

Remember, our fight is not first against flesh and blood but against the powers of darkness.

> Put on the full armor of God, so that you will be able to stand firm against the schemes of the devil. For our struggle is not against flesh and blood, but against

the rulers, against the powers, against the world forces
of this darkness, against the spiritual forces of wickedness in the heavenly places. Therefore, take up the full
armor of God, so that you will be able to resist in the
evil day, and having done everything, to stand firm.

—Ephesians 6:11–13

I have been blessed to help people get set free of demonic
torment, but I've found that some believers want to receive
prayer for deliverance and then never have to contend with
the enemy again. That is not how life works. Even when
people are delivered from the powers of darkness, they're
still going to have to fight with all their heart, soul, mind,
and strength to maintain that victory because those demons
will try to invade their lives again if they don't fight and
resist with the help of Yahweh Nissi.

Think about what happened to King Saul in 1 Samuel
16. He was being terrorized by a demon, and when the evil
spirit came upon him, Saul would call for David to play the
harp. As David played the harp, the Holy Spirit would move
through the music and drive out the demon, but as soon as
David stopped playing, the demon would return.

That's the way it is with deliverance. If you're just looking
for someone to do it all for you, you're going to be forever
defeated. Each of us must learn how to fight for ourselves to
overcome the power of the enemy in our lives. Seven times in
the Book of Revelation, Yeshua says, "He who overcomes will
inherit these things." (See Revelation 2:7, 11, 17, 26; 3:5, 12, 21.)

If you settle for walking through this life defeated, then
you will be defeated, but Yeshua came to set you free, and "if
the Son makes you free, you will be free indeed" (John 8:36).
Messiah Jesus freed us so we can reign in this life (Rom. 5:17).

I discovered this firsthand as a young man. When I was eighteen years old, I was walking in such defeat I couldn't even look people in the eyes. But when I was twenty years old, Yeshua supernaturally revealed Himself to me. He showed me where His Word says in the Book of Ephesians that I have been raised with Christ and am seated with Him in the heavenly places in Messiah Jesus (Eph. 2:6).

Yeshua showed me that "neither death, nor life, nor angels, nor principalities, nor things present, nor things to come, nor powers, nor height, nor depth, nor any other created thing, will be able to separate us from the love of God, which is in Christ Jesus our Lord" (Rom. 8:38–39). Faith and confidence rose up in me when I read, "In all these things, we overwhelmingly conquer through Him who loved us" (Rom. 8:37). I discovered that because I am born again, the Spirit that raised Messiah Yeshua from the dead lives in me, and because I have God's Spirit within me, I cannot help but overcome.

As I began to understand who I am in Messiah Yeshua, I developed a victor's heart. I began to see myself as a winner, seated at the right hand of Father God with Jesus, just as Ephesians says. When I began to look up as a victor, the darkness broke off me, and by the grace of God working within me I've been able to experience more and more freedom over the years.

Father wants you to access all He has provided for you in His Son. Jesus said, "Behold, I have given you authority to tread on serpents and scorpions, and over all the power of the enemy, and nothing will injure you" (Luke 10:19). Life is a struggle. It's a lot like being in a wrestling match. But Yeshua has given us His power and authority, allowing us to reign on the earth as "a kingdom and priests to our God" (Rev. 5:10).

When you come against the enemy, laboring and fighting in Father God's strength, Yahweh Nissi will cause you to triumph in Messiah Jesus. You will live a victorious life, and "the LORD will make you the head and not the tail" (Deut. 28:13). You will have peace of mind and freedom from doubt, worry, and fear. And you will walk in His abundance and blessings. But you must make up your mind that you're going to fight until you are victorious! You must be like Jacob, who wrestled with God and refused to let go until Yahweh blessed him—which He did!

Are you willing to fight for God's best for your life? Whatever it takes, give yourself no rest until you obtain it. Confess that you are victorious in Yeshua and that victory is your portion. Allow no compromise. Keep fighting in Yahweh Nissi's power and strength, and you will ascend through and above the darkness.

CHAPTER 9

YAHWEH M'KADDESH—THE LORD OUR SANCTIFIER

A S WE HAVE seen in the last several chapters, throughout the Torah and Old Testament, Father God connects His personal name, Yahweh, to the functions of the salvation He performs in and for His elect. Another example of this is in the Book of Leviticus where He reveals Himself as *Yahweh M'Kaddesh*, the Lord who sanctifies us:

> You shall consecrate yourselves therefore and be holy, for I am the LORD your God. You shall keep My statutes and practice them; I am the LORD who sanctifies you [Yahweh M'Kaddesh].
>
> —LEVITICUS 20:7–8

The Hebrew word *kadesh* means "clean," and it is closely related to *kadosh*, which means "holy."[1] To be holy is to be set apart or separated unto God. In this passage Father God is reaching out to His people and telling us that because we are His, we must live worthy by being holy before Him. But neither the Law nor our own efforts can make us holy. By revealing Himself as Yahweh M'Kaddesh, God is saying He is the One who sanctifies us by setting us apart to Himself and making us clean.

Consider, however, that the Lord says, "*You* shall consecrate yourselves therefore and be holy." Though He sanctifies us, God makes it clear that He's not going to do it independently of our cooperation. For sanctification to take place in our lives, we must submit to the process. The Ruach HaKodesh ultimately does the work of washing and renewing us, but we have a part to play.

To consecrate ourselves is to give our lives wholly to the Father. The apostle Paul says in 2 Timothy 2:4, "No soldier in active service entangles himself in the affairs of everyday life, so that he may please the one who enlisted him as a soldier." When soldiers are given an assignment, they typically leave home to travel to their deployment, live on a military base in that new location, and leave the base only when permitted, because their lives are focused on their assignment.

In a similar way, the Lord has chosen us to be a people for Himself, but He wants us to respond to His decision to choose us by consecrating ourselves back to Him. Messiah Jesus said, "You did not choose Me but I chose you, and appointed you that you would go and bear fruit, and that your fruit would remain, so that whatever you ask of the Father in My name He may give to you" (John 15:16). Father God is seeking men and women who will rid their hearts of the things of the world and pursue Him.

As we've seen, the term *holy* gets its meaning from the concept of separateness. God is holy, which is to say He is utterly unique, completely separate, and wholly set apart.

He wasn't created like you and me; He has always been. He is the beginning and the end. He has no cause. He is Elohim, the Creator, and because He is separate and unique, He wants His people to be set apart, separate, and unique to Him. We do this by choosing to obey Him and denying our flesh. As we choose to be separate unto God, He performs a supernatural work within our hearts, sanctifying us and making us holy.

But again, there is a partnership in this. Jesus stands at the door knocking, waiting to dine with us, but we must let Him in to experience that kind of fellowship (Rev. 3:20). God wants to do His part, but we must choose to open our hearts and say yes to Him for His work of grace to be completely effective in our lives.

Too many believers are passively waiting for God to do everything, when Messiah Yeshua said, "Ask, and it will be given to you; seek, and you will find; knock, and it will be opened to you" (Matt. 7:7). If we draw near to God, He will draw near to us (Jas. 4:8). God is waiting for us to seek Him. He's waiting for us to choose to love Him so He can complete His process of sanctification in our lives. God does the work, but our hearts must be aligned with Him.

Years ago God gave me a dream in which I was preaching at a church and right in the middle of my message, the congregation stood up, placed their hands over their hearts, and started reciting the Pledge of Allegiance. Then someone yelled, "They don't want to listen to you anymore!" I was so humiliated that I left the pulpit and went into the restroom. While I was in the restroom, I asked God, "Why did that happen? Where did I fail? What did I do so wrong that the congregation would interrupt the preaching of the

Word of God?" Then the Lord said, "Go back in there and finish." So I went back in and finished my preaching, and afterward I heard a voice say, "You did a good job." Then the dream ended.

When I awoke from the dream, I was deeply grieved because I knew God was trying to reveal something to me. Over the next several days, I prayed for revelation of the dream. Then one morning, the Holy Spirit spoke to me and said, "Kirt, what happened in the dream wasn't due to any shortcoming of yours. I was showing you that My people aren't pursuing Me; they're pursuing the American dream." In other words, when the congregation stood up and placed their hands over their hearts to recite the Pledge of Allegiance, they were indicating that instead of being in pursuit of God's Word, they really wanted the American dream and all the material things of this world.

Then I heard the Holy Spirit say, "Unless My people wake up every morning and commit their lives to Me to sanctify and cleanse them, the best preaching in the world won't be able to help them." Beloved, we must say *yes* to God for His Word and Spirit to penetrate our hearts and make us clean. When we choose to cooperate with Him, the Holy Spirit literally goes to work in our lives to transform us into the image of Messiah Jesus.

The apostle Paul said, "He saved us, not on the basis of deeds which we have done in righteousness, but according to His mercy, by the washing of regeneration and renewing by the Holy Spirit" (Titus 3:5). Father God cleanses us as we yield to Him. A supernatural activity takes place in our lives as we consecrate ourselves to the Lord. But we must choose to cooperate.

We see an example of how the Lord uses our cooperation in the sanctification process in His command concerning the Sabbath.

> The LORD spoke to Moses, saying, "But as for you, speak to the sons of Israel, saying, 'You shall surely observe My sabbaths; for this is a sign between Me and you throughout your generations, that you may know that I am the LORD who sanctifies you [Yahweh M'Kaddesh].'"
> —Exodus 31:12–13

In this passage, the Master of the universe tells us that if we will stop working for one day a week, He will sanctify us. When we take a day to disconnect ourselves from the creation to focus on the Creator, we allow God to align our hearts with His. Yahweh M'Kaddesh doesn't make us observe the Sabbath. We must choose to do so, and in so choosing, we position ourselves to experience God's work of sanctification.

The Sabbath is really about recognizing that God is our Master and Creator. He created the heavens and the earth in six days, and then He rested on the seventh day. This, of course, is not because God was tired and needed to rest but because He was giving you and me, whom He created in His very likeness, a pattern for how to live. When we are obedient to God's command to disconnect from the world one day a week to rest and focus on Him, He brings restoration to our souls. But if we choose to ignore the Sabbath principle, we'll miss out on experiencing the fruit of sanctification that comes from observing it.

Yeshua told us, "The Sabbath was made for man, and not man for the Sabbath" (Mark 2:27). God designed the

Sabbath to be a blessing for us, and that blessing is our sanctification and restoration.

The Process of Sanctification

There are actually two components to Yahweh's sanctification process in our lives.

The first component is legal sanctification. Yeshua paid the price of our sins when He died on the cross. His shed blood washed away our sin, and when we receive Messiah Jesus' gift of salvation, we are legally sanctified and will be able to stand before God forgiven and clean.

The second component is experiential sanctification. This is the continual, lifelong process of being cleansed from the darkness of our souls from the stain of sin. This involves being washed of the wrong thought patterns of our minds and the destructive habits in our lives. Every day we must say yes to Yahweh M'Kaddesh and actively pursue His sanctifying work in our lives. The power of the Holy Spirit that transforms us into the likeness of Yeshua doesn't just fall on us. We experience it as we seek God and cooperate with Him. "But we all, with unveiled face, beholding as in a mirror the glory of the Lord, are being transformed into the same image from glory to glory, just as from the Lord, the Spirit" (2 Cor. 3:18).

There are three ways Yahweh M'Kaddesh accomplishes His cleansing work: the blood of Yeshua, the Word of God, and the working of the Holy Spirit.

1. The blood of Yeshua. Yahweh M'Kaddesh initially sanctifies us by the blood of Yeshua when we become born-again believers in Messiah Jesus, for "the blood of Jesus His Son cleanses us from all sin" (1 John 1:7). This is the legal sanctification spoken of previously. We can't make ourselves holy, but as we draw near to God, He imputes His holiness to us. We are sanctified by virtue of our relationship with Him. "In Him we have redemption through His blood, the forgiveness of our trespasses, according to the riches of His grace" (Eph. 1:7).

2. The Word of God. Yahweh M'Kaddesh also sanctifies us by His Word when we obey it. Again, Leviticus 20:8 says, "You shall keep My statutes and practice them; I am the LORD who sanctifies you."

Hebrews 4:12 says, "The word of God is living and active and sharper than any two-edged sword, and piercing as far as the division of soul and spirit, of both joints and marrow, and able to judge the thoughts and intentions of the heart." God's Word is alive and able to expose the thoughts and intentions of our hearts, thus bringing about sanctification in our lives.

Yahweh sanctifies us not only by His written Word but also by His living Word. Yeshua is the living Word of God who became flesh and dwelled among mankind, and He sanctifies us by the truth He speaks. Yeshua said, "You are already clean because of the word which I have spoken to you" (John 15:3). Messiah Jesus' very words are true and powerful. As you surrender to Yahweh M'Kaddesh to sanctify you, God will speak the truth of His Word to your heart and cleanse you.

3. The Holy Spirit. In addition to being sanctified by the blood of Yeshua and the Word of God, Yahweh M'Kaddesh sanctifies us by the indwelling work of the Holy Spirit. The Ruach HaKodesh is alive within us, and He can literally change our nature, as the prophet Ezekiel proclaimed:

> Moreover, I will give you a new heart and put a new spirit within you; and I will remove the heart of stone

> from your flesh and give you a heart of flesh. I will put
> My Spirit within you and cause you to walk in My stat-
> utes, and you will be careful to observe My ordinances.
> —Ezekiel 36:26–27

Father God places His Spirit within us, removing our hard hearts and replacing them with hearts that are soft and sensitive to Him. Just as leopards cannot change their spots (Jer. 13:23) so are we incapable of changing our own hearts. Only the Holy Spirit can do this. Paul said, "But you were washed, but you were sanctified, but you were justified in the name of the Lord Jesus Christ *and in the Spirit of our God*" (1 Cor. 6:11). Yahweh M'Kaddesh washes and sanctifies us by the supernatural work of the indwelling Holy Spirit. "He saved us…by the washing of regeneration and renewing by the Holy Spirit" (Titus 3:5).

Called to Be Holy

God leads us through the process of sanctification because He has called us to be holy as He is holy. God has many attributes. He is loving, peace giving, forgiving, all-knowing, all-powerful, and many other things, but above all else, He is holy. In fact, there are only two times in the entire Bible, both the Old and New Testaments, where we find a three-fold repetition of any of God's attributes. We often see a twofold repetition of God's attributes, but only twice in the Scriptures do we find a threefold repetition of God's attributes, and it's only in connection with His holiness.

The Bible records two visions in which God is seen sitting on the throne in heaven. One of these visions was seen by the apostle John on the island of Patmos and the other by the prophet Isaiah. In these visions, John and Isaiah see the same thing. They see God sitting on His throne in heaven with divine beings surrounding Him, crying out day and night, "Holy, holy, holy."

> Immediately I was in the Spirit; and behold, a throne was standing in heaven, and One sitting on the throne.... And the four living creatures, each one of them having six wings, are full of eyes around and within; and day and night they do not cease to say, "Holy, holy, holy is the LORD God, the Almighty, who was and who is and who is to come."
>
> —REVELATION 4:2, 8

> In the year of King Uzziah's death I saw the Lord sitting on a throne, lofty and exalted, with the train of His robe filling the temple. Seraphim stood above Him, each having six wings: with two he covered his face, and with two he covered his feet, and with two he flew. And one called out to another and said, "Holy, Holy, Holy, is the LORD of hosts, the whole earth is full of His glory." And the foundations of the thresholds trembled at the voice of him who called out, while the temple was filling with smoke. Then I said, "Woe is me, for I am ruined! Because I am a man of unclean lips, and I live among a people of unclean lips; for my eyes have seen the King, the LORD of hosts."
>
> Then one of the seraphim flew to me with a burning coal in his hand, which he had taken from the altar with tongs. He touched my mouth with it and said, "Behold, this has touched your lips; and your iniquity is taken away and your sin is forgiven." Then I heard the voice of the Lord, saying, "Whom shall I send, and who will go for Us?" Then I said, "Here am I. Send me!"
>
> —ISAIAH 6:1–8

When Isaiah saw the vision of God on the throne, he was overwhelmed by God's holiness, and it pained him to realize how unclean he himself was. Isaiah lived in a culture that was completely impure, and he recognized that he had become too much like those around him. Father God called Isaiah to be sanctified and holy, completely different from the world around him. In desperation and agony Isaiah cried out to the Lord, and in return Yahweh M'Kaddesh touched Isaiah's lips with a burning coal, sanctifying him; then He commissioned Isaiah as a prophet to the nations.

The Lord is calling you and me as He did Isaiah to be holy and set apart for Him. The truth is, if you have accepted Messiah Jesus as your Savior, you are a priest, and you need to start thinking of yourself as one. Revelation 5:10 says as followers of Yeshua, we have been made "a kingdom and priests to our God," and Father God always sanctified His priests. In Exodus 30, God instructed Moses to "anoint Aaron and his sons, and consecrate them, that they may minister as priests to Me" (v. 30).

If you desire to fulfill God's calling in your life, you must recognize that you are a priest and be serious about your sanctification. Too many of God's people don't realize that when they allow all the things of the world to penetrate them, they are actually aborting God's purposes for their lives.

Several years ago the Lord spoke to me and said, "Seize My Word and don't let anything else in." We must continually focus on God and His Word, keeping out all the things of the world that will pollute us and bring destruction in our lives. When we're deciding what to watch on television, our decision shouldn't first be based on what we like but on whether Father God would be pleased with us watching that show.

The filter for every decision we make should be, "Does this please You, Lord?" When we are engaged in a conversation, we need to ask, "Does this conversation please You, Lord?" When we're listening to a song, we need to ask, "Does this song please You, Father God?" When we're involved in a relationship, we need to ask, "Does this relationship please You, Lord?"

If we desire to walk in the fullness of God's blessings and the sanctification process Yahweh M'Kaddesh desires to work in our lives, we must choose to cut off everything in our hearts that doesn't sanctify Him as Lord. Of course we'll never be totally sanctified until we're in heaven with Yeshua, but that doesn't mean we shouldn't do our best to love God with all our heart, mind, soul, and strength and allow Him to change us here and now.

The Lord called for the nation of Israel to be holy, saying, "You shall be holy, for I the LORD your God am holy" (Lev. 19:2). God has not changed His mind. The apostle Peter wrote, "Like the Holy One who called you, be holy yourselves also in all your behavior; because it is written, 'You shall be holy, for I am holy'" (1 Pet. 1:15–16).

As previously stated, the Hebrew word for holy, *kadosh*, means to be completely different, wholly other, totally unique, and set apart. God wants His people to be set apart and completely different from the world. This is why Yahweh gave the nation of Israel specific instructions in the Torah that completely separated them from the surrounding nations.

For example, in Leviticus 11, Elohim gave precise guidelines for what the Israelites were to eat. The Hebrew word *kashruth* refers to this set of Jewish dietary laws, and the English word *kosher* refers to food that is in accordance with Jewish law. Although there are health benefits to eating kosher, the rabbis agree that the primary reason God gave these dietary regulations was not for the health benefits but for the purpose of sanctification. He wanted to separate Israel from all the other nations of the world.

When Daniel was exiled to Babylon, he asked permission to eat only vegetables instead of the king's choice food and to drink only water instead of the king's choice wine (Dan. 1:8–14). Daniel desired to be sanctified before God, and God used him as a mighty prophetic voice to accomplish His purposes.

Yahweh M'Kaddesh cares about every part of our lives. The Scriptures say: "Do you not know that your body is a temple of the Holy Spirit who is in you, whom you have from God, and that you are not your own? For you have been bought with a price: therefore glorify God in your body" (1 Cor. 6:19–20). Father God wants us to live with the awareness that our bodies are the temple of the Holy Spirit, and we should treat them as such.

Many of God's children are destroying their bodies by overeating. If you need discipline in the area of your eating habits, keep crying out to Yahweh M'Kaddesh for help and sanctification, and He will bring your eating habits into the conformity of His will. He dealt with the nation of Israel about their dietary choices, and He cares about ours as well.

God also gave the Israelites specific instructions in the Torah regarding how they were to dress. He said, "You shall not wear a material mixed of wool and linen together" (Deut. 22:11). Many Bible scholars believe God commanded the children of Israel not to mix those fabrics because the heathen nations around them wore garments mixed of wool and linen and the Lord wanted Israel to look completely different from all the other nations.

Yahweh also told the children of Israel how their hair was to be worn, saying, "You shall not round off the side-growth of your heads nor harm the edges of your beard" (Lev. 19:27). Why would Father God care how His people cut their hair? Again, He wanted them to stand out as His unique, cut-out, separated people.

Beloved, the Lord wants us to be different from the world, even in the way we dress. He doesn't want us to look like the secular world. Women shouldn't wear clothes that are designed to draw attention to their bodies, creating a snare for the men of God's kingdom, and men shouldn't wear clothes that draw attention to their flesh. We must dress in a way that shows modesty and holiness, presenting ourselves as priests of Yeshua. This doesn't mean we shouldn't or can't dress attractively but rather that our dress should be appropriate for God's sons and daughters.

God also cares how we steward our finances. The Lord told the people of Israel, "Thus all the tithe of the land, of the seed of the land or of the fruit of the tree, is the LORD's; it is holy to the LORD" (Lev. 27:30). If you're not tithing to God, you might consider that there's a problem with sanctification in your life. Often the reason people don't tithe is they're living to please themselves and not Father God.

The Torah addresses these issues that to some may seem offensive and to others insignificant, but God wants to bring *every* area of our lives under His obedience and into sanctification. He desires to sanctify us fully and completely. This is why Paul prayed, "Now may the God of peace Himself sanctify you entirely; and may your spirit and soul and body be preserved complete, without blame at the coming of our Lord Jesus" (1 Thess. 5:23).

We've been created in God's image, and as believers in Yeshua, we too are called to be holy just as He is holy. Even as God called the Israelites to be His people, so you are part of a chosen remnant. If you are a follower of Messiah Yeshua, it is because the Lord specifically chose you out of the world to be His. The Scriptures tell us no one can come to Yeshua unless the Father draws him (John 6:44, 65), so if you are a believer in Messiah Jesus, God in His loving-kindness literally chose you to be His.

The apostle Paul wrote that Father God *"chose us in Him before the foundation of the world*, that we would be holy and blameless before Him. In love He predestined us to adoption as sons through Jesus Christ to Himself, according to the kind intention of His will"* (Eph. 1:3–5). Peter wrote, "You are a chosen race, a royal priesthood, a holy nation, a people for God's own possession, so that you may proclaim the excellencies of Him who has called you out of darkness into His marvelous light" (1 Pet. 2:9).

When you understand that God loves you and has chosen you to be His by revealing Himself to you and giving you faith in Him, you'll be so blessed and thankful that you'll be willing to say yes to the sanctification process, and your burning desire will be to seek Him, not the American dream. You'll be willing to say, "I don't care if I lose the world as long as I can gain You, Lord. You are my exceedingly great reward, the pearl of great price, and in You are all the treasures of life!"

Are You Willing to Pay the Price?

We've not only been chosen to reign with Yeshua, but we've also been chosen to suffer for His sake. The Bible tells us:

> If we suffer, we shall also reign with him.
>
> —2 Timothy 2:12, kjv

> For to you it has been granted for Christ's sake, not only to believe in Him, but also to suffer for His sake.
>
> —Philippians 1:29

There is a price for being different from the world, and if we want to walk in sanctification, we must be willing to pay it. We can't say on one hand that we desire God and on the other hand so fear rejection by the world that we do everything we can to fit in with the culture around us. We can't have it both ways. James warned us about this, saying, "Do you not know that friendship with the world is hostility toward God? Therefore whoever wishes to be a friend of the world makes himself an enemy of God" (Jas. 4:4).

As children of God, we must be willing to be rejected. Yeshua said: "If the world hates you, you know that it has hated Me before it hated you. If you were of the world, the world would love its own; but because you are not of the world, but I chose you out of the world, because of this the world hates you" (John 15:18–19). So if the world's culture loves us, if we fit right in with it so that no one notices we're of a different spirit with different values and ways of thinking, the obvious implication is that we're of the world. If we find ourselves mixing in perfectly with the world and its culture, there's a serious problem with our sanctification.

When Yeshua died on the cross, He was crucified outside the gates of Jerusalem, a place of shame reserved for criminals. We too must suffer with Him by going "out to Him outside the camp, bearing His reproach" (Heb. 13:13).

Beloved, if you're not willing to pay the price of sanctification, you must ask yourself if you truly have a saving relationship with God. Remember, Yeshua says not everyone who says to Him, "Lord, Lord," will enter the kingdom of heaven, but only those who do the will of the Father (Matt. 7:21).

Messiah Jesus tells us in Matthew 7:13–14:

> Enter through the narrow gate; for the gate is wide and the way is broad that leads to destruction, and there are many who enter through it. For the gate is small and the way is narrow that leads to life, and there are few who find it.

We must choose which path to follow in life. The first gate Yeshua described is one of self-pleasure; it's wide, and most walk through it. It leads to destruction and death. The second gate is one of self-denial for Yeshua's sake. This gate is narrow, and few find it, but it leads to eternal life.

Salvation is a free gift of God, but it entails being willing to endure conflict, persecution, and even death for Yeshua's sake. This is why Jesus said:

> And he who does not take his cross and follow after Me is not worthy of Me. He who has found his life will lose it, and he who has lost his life for My sake will find it.
> —Matthew 10:38–39

Messiah Jesus tells us He will spit out of His mouth those who are lukewarm toward Him (Rev. 3:15–16). God is calling you and me to be on fire for Him. He's calling you to be radically different from the world. This is why I love to be called a Jesus freak. To me, there's no higher privilege. When I'm rejected for identifying with Messiah Yeshua, I'm blessed and thankful because it's truly a privilege to be rejected for His sake.

It comes down to this: Are you willing to pay the price for Yahweh M'Kaddesh to bring sanctification to your life? Are you willing to say no to the world and yes to the Lord? Are you ready to say, "I don't care what anyone thinks or says; I don't care what relationships need to end; I'm willing to pay the price no matter what it costs me because deep in my heart, I love You, Jesus, and I have a passion to fulfill Your call in my life, which is to know You, love You, experience You, walk with You, and be conformed to Your image"?

Yahweh M'Kaddesh is ready to release His power into our lives, but He's waiting for us to open our hearts to Him, deny the things of the world that corrupt us, and say yes to Him. As we do, we're going to be transformed into the likeness of Yeshua, and others will see His power and glory shining more and more brightly through our lives.

Let's invite Yahweh M'Kaddesh to come into our lives and sanctify our hearts and souls through the Ruach HaKodesh. He disciplines every soul He loves. "'For those whom the Lord loves He disciplines, and He scourges every son whom He receives.' …All discipline for the moment seems not to be joyful, but sorrowful; yet to those who have been trained by it, afterwards it yields the peaceful fruit of righteousness" (Heb. 12:6, 11). His cleansing is truly a beautiful thing!

CHAPTER 10

YAHWEH SHALOM—THE LORD OUR PEACE

MOST PEOPLE ARE familiar with the Hebrew word *shalom*, which means peace. In Israel, *shalom* is such a highly valued word it is used both to say hello and goodbye. But biblically speaking, *shalom* refers to much more than a pleasant greeting or even the absence of conflict. It means complete wholeness, restoration, and fullness—spirit, soul, mind, and body. When Father God revealed Himself as Yahweh Shalom, this is what He was promising His people—to bring us into a state where we are whole and complete in Him.

We see how completely God is committed to blessing us with His shalom in the Aaronic Blessing: "The LORD bless you, and keep you; the LORD make His face shine on you, and be gracious to you; the LORD lift up His countenance on you, and give you peace [shalom]" (Num. 6:24–26).

We never have to doubt whether Father God wants us to walk in His peace. Not only does He make this known through the Aaronic Blessing; it is evident in His very name, Yahweh Shalom, "the Lord our Peace."

Gideon and the God of Peace

The Lord declared Himself Yahweh Shalom in only one place in Scripture: Judges 6. At this point in their history the Israelites were in a vicious cycle of trusting Yahweh, then turning their hearts to false gods, then returning to the Lord, only to abandon Him again. Because of their rebellion, the Lord allowed them to be severely oppressed by the Midianites for seven years.

Whenever the people of Israel sowed grain, the Midianites would swoop in and destroy their produce, leaving them neither wheat nor livestock. The Scriptures say these adversaries "would come in like locusts for number, both they and their camels were innumerable; and they came into the land to devastate it" (Judg. 6:5).

Then one day the angel of the Lord appeared to a man named Gideon as he was beating wheat in a winepress. Take that in for a moment. In an attempt to hide his grain, Gideon was threshing wheat in a place designed for winemaking. That's how desperate he was.

Gideon was discouraged when the Lord appeared to him:

> The angel of the LORD appeared to him and said to him, "The LORD is with you, O valiant warrior." Then Gideon said to him, "O my lord, if the LORD is with us, why then has all this happened to us? And where are all His miracles which our fathers told us about, saying, 'Did not the LORD bring us up from Egypt?' But now the LORD has abandoned us and given us into the hand of Midian."
>
> —JUDGES 6:12–13

The Israelites had been suffering under the hands of their enemies, and like many of us, Gideon wondered why God was letting these bad things happen. He had heard of Yahweh Nissi's great exploits in the past, and Gideon wanted to know where God's power was now. Where were the miracles he'd heard about?

He wasn't expecting this response from his God:

> The LORD looked at him and said, "Go in this your strength and deliver Israel from the hand of Midian. Have I not sent you?"
>
> —JUDGES 6:14

Gideon was being raised up to deliver Israel, but he didn't feel like much of a valiant warrior; he felt weak and inferior.

> He said to Him, "O Lord, how shall I deliver Israel? Behold, my family is the least in Manasseh, and I am the youngest in my father's house." But the LORD said to him, "Surely I will be with you, and you shall defeat Midian as one man."
>
> —JUDGES 6:15–16

Even though the Lord promised to be with him, Gideon was still filled with doubt and confusion. His family was the least in his clan, and he was the youngest in his father's house. Gideon didn't see how he could be the one called to defeat the Midianites, and he needed some reassurance.

> So Gideon said to Him, "If now I have found favor in Your sight, then show me a sign that it is You who speak with me. Please do not depart from here, until I come back to You, and bring out my offering and lay it before You." And He said, "I will remain until you return."

> Then Gideon went in and prepared a young goat and unleavened bread from an ephah of flour; he put the meat in a basket and the broth in a pot, and brought them out to him under the oak and presented them. The angel of God said to him, "Take the meat and the unleavened bread and lay them on this rock, and pour out the broth." And he did so. Then the angel of the LORD put out the end of the staff that was in his hand and touched the meat and the unleavened bread; and fire sprang up from the rock and consumed the meat and the unleavened bread. Then the angel of the LORD vanished from his sight.
>
> When Gideon saw that he was the angel of the LORD, he said, "Alas, O Lord GOD! For now I have seen the angel of the LORD face to face."
>
> —JUDGES 6:17–22

Gideon asked for a sign that the angel was really of God, but seeing the food he prepared be miraculously consumed by fire filled Gideon with holy awe! He knew he had seen the Lord! We know Gideon didn't simply encounter an angel because the word *Lord* in reference to the angel of the Lord is rendered in capital letters. This means it is the Hebrew letters *yod, hey, vav, hey,* which is God's personal name, Yahweh. The angel that Gideon saw wasn't Michael or Gabriel; it was likely a preincarnate manifestation of Messiah Jesus.

I love what happened next.

> The LORD said to him, "Peace to you, do not fear; you shall not die." Then Gideon built an altar there to the LORD and named it The LORD is Peace [Yahweh Shalom].
>
> —JUDGES 6:23–24

The Lord addressed Gideon's fear, and His words brought such assurance and peace to Gideon's heart that he built an altar there and named the place "The Lord Is Peace." He went on to do great exploits for God, defeating the vast Midianite army with only three hundred soldiers. He did it because he was filled with the supernatural power that came from Yahweh's shalom.

Beloved, God is still silencing doubt and confusion and raising up men and women to do mighty exploits for His kingdom. If you trust Him, Yahweh Shalom will fill your heart with courage, just as He did for Gideon. It often takes time and experience, but as we persevere with Yahweh Shalom, we will absolutely grow in stability and freedom through His supernatural peace.

We never have to wonder whether Father God wants to give us peace. He said through the prophet Isaiah, "For the mountains may be removed and the hills may shake, but My lovingkindness will not be removed from you, and My covenant of peace will not be shaken" (Isa. 54:10). Yahweh Shalom has made a covenant of peace with His people through Messiah Jesus, and it is forever His will that you and I should have peace.

Yeshua—the Sar Shalom

Yeshua, Yahweh's Son, is the *Sar Shalom*, the Prince of Peace. In his beautiful prophecy of the coming Messiah, Isaiah declared:

> For a child will be born to us, a son will be given to us; and the government will rest on His shoulders; and His name will be called Wonderful Counselor, Mighty God, Eternal Father, *Prince of Peace* [Sar Shalom].
>
> —ISAIAH 9:6

Messiah Jesus said, "Come to Me, all who are weary and heavy-laden, and I will give you rest" (Matt. 11:28). In another passage Yeshua said, "My peace I give to you; not as the world gives do I give to you" (John 14:27). The peace Yeshua gives is unlike anything we will find in the world. He fills us with an abiding inner peace that is independent of our circumstances.

Too often we seek peace in things outside ourselves. This is what I call external peace, and we can only experience it in an environment where we have absolutely no problems. This kind of peace is totally dependent on our circumstances, and because our circumstances are constantly changing, this peace never lasts. Internal peace, on the other hand, is a deep, abiding peace within. It's not at all dependent upon our circumstances; it's from the realm of eternity.

Only through Yeshua, the Sar Shalom, can we experience peace that "surpasses all comprehension" (Phil. 4:7). Jesus didn't promise His disciples lives free from trouble. Rather, He promised them His peace. Yeshua said, "These things I have spoken to you, so that in Me you may have peace. In the world you have tribulation, but take courage; I have overcome the world" (John 16:33).

The Sar Shalom carried within Him a tranquility that was independent of His circumstances. Because of the tremendous, incredible, unconquerable peace within Him, He was able to rebuke the wind and waves of a great storm on the Sea of Galilee, and when He spoke, immediately the storm settled and the sea became perfectly calm (Matt. 8:23–27). The peace inside Yeshua overcame the storm raging all around Him. This is what we need, a peace that keeps us whole despite our circumstances.

Paul wrote, "The God of peace will soon crush Satan under your feet" (Rom. 16:20). The spirit of Satan, of course, is the exact opposite of the true spirit of peace. He torments us with strife and chaos, while the God of peace brings stability and order to our lives.

In the Book of Revelation, the apostle John saw a vision of heaven in which God was sitting on a throne. John said, "Before the throne there was something like a sea of glass, like crystal" (Rev. 4:6). Why did John describe this *sea of glass*? Why was it such an important detail to mention? Consider that glass is perfectly flat; there are no waves or ripples in it. This sea of glass in heaven speaks of an absolute stillness, where there are no ripples of worry, anxiety, or fear. It is a picture of the perfect peace that Father God through Yeshua gives us as we draw near to Him.

In fact, peace is one of the primary gifts God desires to give us. When Yeshua appeared to His disciples after He had risen from the dead, He came into their midst and said, "Peace be with you." Then He breathed on them and said, "Receive the Holy Spirit" (John 20:21–22).

Peace is a fruit of the Spirit (Gal. 5:22–23). Many times when people think of the gifts of the Holy Spirit, they think of the more sensational charismatic gifts such as speaking in tongues, but He confers a deeper, wider, fuller, more permanent and foundational gift, and that is peace.

How do we walk in the peace of God? The Bible says, "You will keep him in perfect peace, whose mind is stayed on You, because he trusts in You" (Isa. 26:3, MEV). Trusting Yeshua, the Sar Shalom, enables us to walk in His peace and overcome the enemy.

It's also important that we get quiet if we want to

experience God's peace. In 1 Kings 19, the prophet Elijah is on the run from the wicked queen Jezebel and is hiding in a cave at Mount Sinai in need of a word from God. The Lord instructs Elijah to stand on the mountain because He is going to pass by. A strong wind starts breaking the rocks of the mountain into pieces, but the Lord is not in the wind. After the wind, there is an earthquake, but He is not in the earthquake. After the earthquake, there is a fire, but God is not in the fire. After the fire, there is the sound of a still, small voice. In this instance, Elijah didn't find Father God in the sensational—the wind, the earthquake, or the fire; he found Him in a still, small voice. He found the Lord in peace.

It's so important that we intentionally and with discipline still ourselves before the Lord to find peace. People pursue many things in this world—knowledge, money, and social status, just to name a few. But one of our top priorities in life should be pursuing peace.

To experience peace, we must come out of the world and spend time being still before God, quietly waiting on Him. The Bible tells us, "Be still, and know that I am God" (Ps. 46:10, NIV). Our lives are so busy. We're doing so many things that we just don't take the time to be still before God. If we stop running here and there and take the time to sit quietly before God, not allowing the things of the world to distract us, God will be able to impart His peace within us.

One night I had a dream that brought this truth into sharp focus. In the dream, I found myself sitting in a dark room across from a man I knew was a familiar friend who had been with me a long time. But I soon grew tired of sitting across from this man and wanted to leave the room because nothing seemed to be happening. I was bored and wanted to do something more exciting.

When the dream ended, the Lord revealed to me that the man in the dream was Yeshua. He said, "It may seem like nothing's happening sometimes. It may feel boring and uncomfortable, but if you will just sit quietly before Me every day, waiting on Me, you will experience greater and greater peace and be made whole." Instead of leaving to do something more exciting or stimulating, I needed to sit still before God.

Lees pog is a Hebrew term that means to soak up. When you spend time in *lees pog*, you are simply sitting before the Lord, resting and soaking in His presence. Many of us need the self-discipline to sit quietly before God. Some people feel a constant need to be talking with others. It's impossible to have peace if you're always talking. If you constantly need to be stimulated from the outside, you'll never be able to sense Yahweh Shalom within you, and you'll never experience His peace.

If you remember the story of Mary and Martha in Luke 10, you'll recall that Martha was busy preparing the meal while Mary simply sat at Yeshua's feet to receive from Him. Martha became upset at Mary because she wasn't helping her with all the meal preparations. But when Martha complained to Messiah Jesus, He said, "Martha, Martha...you are worried and upset about many things, but few things are needed—or indeed only one. Mary has chosen what is better, and it will not be taken away from her" (Luke 10:41–42, NIV).

What Martha was doing was important. I can't imagine what a privilege it would be to serve Yeshua by preparing a meal for Him. Yet Jesus said Mary had chosen what was better by deciding to simply sit at His feet to receive from Him. Beloved, we need to become more like Mary. We must daily place ourselves in a posture of simply sitting before the Lord and waiting to receive from Him.

Discovering the Peace of God

Several years ago, I had spent about a year praying for Father God to give me more peace. Then one night I had a profound dream that I knew was from the Lord. Some dreams are just our minds processing our life experiences, and some come from the enemy. But I knew this dream came from the Spirit of God.

In the dream I found myself in the most beautiful, lush forest you could ever imagine. The forest was surrounded by rock formations covered with thick ivy, making it a secret, secluded paradise. As I beheld the beauty of this forest, the Spirit of God kept covering me in billows of peace. I literally felt my soul being filled with the peace of God; it was the most emotionally satisfying experience I'd ever had. I continued to feel wave after wave of God's presence and peace as He led me deeper and deeper into the forest.

Deep in the center of the forest there was a simple wooden picnic table, which I knew represented God's fullness and abundance. As the Spirit of God drew me deeper into the forest toward the picnic table, I suddenly smelled pizza in my dream. This was the best-smelling pizza I'd ever encountered, and the scent was so strong it made me hungry, even though I hadn't been hungry before I smelled it. I became immediately distracted, and I didn't know what to do.

On one hand, I wanted to follow the Spirit of God deeper into the forest toward the picnic table to experience more of His supernatural peace, but on the other hand, I desired the pizza. I wanted both! Then I yielded to my flesh and thought, "Maybe I can have a piece of pizza and then follow God's Spirit deeper into the forest."

As soon as that thought entered my mind, the dream was over, and God's peace left me. I was so grieved! This encounter with God was one of the most incredible, emotionally satisfying experiences I'd ever had, and I traded it for a lousy piece of pizza.

I got out of bed, fell on my knees, and cried out: "God, forgive me. I can't believe I did that. I've been praying for an entire year for Your peace in my life, and I traded it for a lousy piece of pizza." Then I sensed the Lord say, "If you'll deny yourself the natural, then you'll be drawn deeper into the supernatural, and you'll experience more of My glory and My peace." I knew the Lord was telling me that if I wanted more peace, I'd have to deny my flesh and feed my spirit.

If you earnestly seek Father God for His peace, I promise He will give it to you. True, lasting peace will never be found on the outside. Peace that is rooted in circumstances will never last because our circumstances are constantly changing, but the peace of God is solid and enduring. Just as Yeshua, the Sar Shalom, calmed the storm on the Sea of Galilee for His disciples, He can calm any storm that comes in your life. The same Spirit of peace that quieted the wind and waves is within you. When you receive the Holy Spirit as a believer in Messiah Jesus, you receive the same impartation of peace Yeshua gave when He breathed on His disciples.

Beloved, I challenge you to take the time to feed your spirit. If you do this out of love for God, Yahweh Shalom is going to build you up, because when you sow to the Spirit, you're going to reap from the Spirit love, joy, and peace.

CHAPTER 11

YAHWEH ROHI—THE LORD OUR SHEPHERD

O F ALL THE ways Father God has revealed Himself to us, one of the most familiar is as Yahweh Rohi, "the Lord our Shepherd." The Hebrew word *rohi* comes from the root *rāʿâ* (or *raah*), which means to tend or feed. This is what Father God does for us. He is the Good Shepherd who lovingly cares for us, protects us, and meets our needs.

This image of God as a compassionate shepherd tending His sheep is seen throughout the Scriptures. The prophet Isaiah declared, "Like a shepherd He will tend His flock, in His arm He will gather the lambs and carry them in His bosom; He will gently lead the nursing ewes" (Isa. 40:11).

And the Lord said through the prophet Ezekiel:

"Behold, I Myself will search for My sheep and seek them out. As a shepherd cares for his herd in the day when he is among his scattered sheep, so I will care for My sheep and will deliver them from all the places to which they were scattered on a cloudy and gloomy day. I will bring

them out from the peoples and gather them from the
countries and bring them to their own land; and I will
feed them on the mountains of Israel, by the streams,
and in all the inhabited places of the land. I will feed
them in a good pasture, and their grazing ground will
be on the mountain heights of Israel. There they will lie
down on good grazing ground and feed in rich pasture
on the mountains of Israel. I will feed My flock and I
will lead them to rest," declares the Lord God.

—Ezekiel 34:11–15

The Lord promises to be a Good Shepherd who will
gather His sheep to Himself and lead them to good ground,
where they will be safe and find rest. The same theme flows
into the B'rit Hadashah, the New Testament, where Yeshua
says of Himself:

I am the good shepherd; the good shepherd lays down
His life for the sheep. He who is a hired hand, and not
a shepherd, who is not the owner of the sheep, sees the
wolf coming, and leaves the sheep and flees, and the
wolf snatches them and scatters them. He flees because
he is a hired hand and is not concerned about the sheep.

—John 10:11–13

In the Book of Revelation, the apostle John wrote that
after the tribulation, a great multitude from every nation,
people, and tongue will stand before the throne of God. And
"the Lamb in the center of the throne will be their shepherd,
and will guide them to springs of the water of life; and God
will wipe every tear from their eyes" (Rev. 7:17).

Seeing God as a caring shepherd is clearly an important
theme in Scripture, but why did God use this image to reveal
Himself to His people? Tending livestock was, of course, a

common occupation in biblical times, and the responsibilities and burdens of a shepherd would have been familiar to the ancient Israelites. When the Lord revealed Himself as Yahweh Rohi, the people of Israel understood their God was communicating that He would protect and care for them.

A shepherd's life was neither easy nor glamorous. They had to constantly watch the sheep, sometimes sleeping outdoors to protect the flock from thieves and predators.

But I don't believe God likened Himself to a shepherd solely because it painted a familiar picture for His people. There's also no denying the ancient Israelites behaved a lot like sheep in need of a shepherd, as do we today. Sheep aren't the brightest animals and need constant guidance. They are prone to wandering and often can't find their way even when the shepherd is in view.[1] Does that sound familiar? Isaiah declared, "All of us like sheep have gone astray, each of us has turned to his own way; but the LORD has caused the iniquity of us all to fall on Him" (Isa. 53:6).

Like sheep, we have a tendency to go off course, following our own fleshly desires and trusting our wisdom over Father God's. Too often we lose sight of what God has promised in His Word and begin to doubt that we can fully rely on the Master of the universe. But as our Shepherd, Yahweh Rohi is always here to patiently guide us. If we follow Him, He will lead us by His Spirit into the good future He has planned for us.

We see this most clearly in Psalm 23, written by David, the great king of Israel who was once a shepherd himself. He knew from personal experience exactly what a shepherd does to care and provide for his sheep. In David's famous psalm, Father God reveals Himself as Yahweh Rohi, the

Lord our Shepherd, giving the most tender and specific details of what exactly this means for you and me.

David wrote in Psalm 23:

> The LORD is my shepherd, I shall not want. He makes me lie down in green pastures; He leads me beside quiet waters. He restores my soul; He guides me in the paths of righteousness for His name's sake. Even though I walk through the valley of the shadow of death, I fear no evil, for You are with me; Your rod and Your staff, they comfort me. You prepare a table before me in the presence of my enemies; You have anointed my head with oil; My cup overflows. Surely goodness and lovingkindness will follow me all the days of my life, and I will dwell in the house of the LORD forever.

First, notice that David says the Lord *is* our Shepherd. Yahweh is alive and active in our lives here and now. This psalm isn't telling us the Lord *was* our Shepherd; it's letting us know He is currently involved in our lives. As we saw in chapter 4, the name Yahweh is not a noun in the traditional sense; it communicates continuous, unfinished action. Yahweh Rohi is always present in our lives and acting as our Shepherd as we look to Him and respond to His Word in obedience.

God is the same yesterday, today, and forever, and what He did for David in Psalm 23, He does for you and me today as we open our lives to Him.

Yahweh Rohi Provides for Us

The first line of David's psalm tells us that because the Lord is our Shepherd, we shall not want. We can trust that our God will provide everything we need. That doesn't mean

He will give us everything we want. God is gracious and blesses us with many gifts, but He knows what we need. So while He may not give us everything we could ever wish for, He will provide for our true needs.

Messiah Jesus said:

> Do not be worried about your life, as to what you will eat or what you will drink; nor for your body, as to what you will put on. Is not life more than food, and the body more than clothing? Look at the birds of the air, that they do not sow, nor reap nor gather into barns, and yet your heavenly Father feeds them. Are you not worth much more than they?
>
> —MATTHEW 6:25–26

We don't need to worry about what is going to become of us in our old age. We don't have to worry about where we will end up in life or how we're going to survive as our world continues to become a darker and more dangerous place. Our God is going to take care of us. Yahweh Rohi will provide.

Yahweh Rohi Gives Us Rest

David goes on to say Yahweh Rohi makes us lie down in green pastures and leads us beside still waters. This imagery speaks of peace and rest.

The Bible says in Hebrews 11:6, "And without faith it is impossible to please Him, for he who comes to God must believe that He is and that He is a rewarder of those who seek Him." Beloved, if we're going to walk with God and truly experience Him as Yahweh Rohi, we must believe He is who He says He is and will do what He says He will do.

Father God has promised to give us peace and rest. Let's anchor ourselves in that promise.

> Therefore, let us fear if, while a promise remains of entering His rest, any one of you may seem to have come short of it....Therefore let us be diligent to enter that rest, so that no one will fall, through following the same example of disobedience.
>
> —Hebrews 4:1, 11

Entering God's rest involves getting strong in the Spirit. Believe you can have rest. Believe you can have peace. And don't stop asking, seeking, and knocking until you enter into it. This is progressive, but the key is to live from the inside out. We have to draw our focus from outside ourselves to instead keep our focus on Jesus, who is reigning at the Father's right hand in the heavenly places, and fellowship with Him by abiding in His Spirit within.

As we mature in this, we will better be able to discern the Lord's will, but it is not enough to simply discern His will. We must obey. The more we abide in Him through obedience, the more rest we will have. Jesus said, "He who has My commandments and keeps them is the one who loves Me; and he who loves Me will be loved by My Father, and I will love him and will disclose Myself to him" (John 14:21).

This verse confused me for many years because it sounds like we're earning God's love through obedience when in fact we know that God's love is unconditional, and this is why Jesus died for us while we were yet sinners (Rom. 5:8). Eventually, after struggling to understand this concept of being loved by the Father as we obey Him, I understood that what Jesus was referring to is an experiential consciousness of the Father's love that comes to us as we obey. In other words, His love for us never changes, but we cannot enjoy it unless we obey Him. As we continue to pray, obey, and fellowship with God through the Holy Spirit, we will become strong and whole and enter His rest. We are on a quest.

Yahweh Rohi Heals and Restores Us

In verse 3 of Psalm 23, David says, "He restores my soul." Many people have wounds in their souls that are keeping them from moving forward in life. Some are afraid to trust because of past betrayal or abuse. Others have a hard time maintaining relationships because they are still suffering the pain of divorce or an abusive parent. The world says time heals all wounds. The truth is that time doesn't heal everything, but Yeshua does. No matter what you've been through, the Lord can and will restore your soul.

When Messiah Jesus began His public ministry, one of the first things He did was go into the synagogue and read on the Sabbath.

> The scroll of the prophet Isaiah was handed to Him. When He had unrolled the scroll, He found the place where it was written: "The Spirit of the Lord is upon Me, because He has anointed Me to preach the gospel to the poor; He has sent Me to heal the broken-hearted, to preach deliverance to the captives and recovery of sight to the blind, to set at liberty those who are oppressed; to preach the acceptable year of the Lord." Then He rolled up the scroll, and He gave it back to the attendant, and sat down. The eyes of all those who were in the synagogue were fixed on Him. And He began to say to them, "Today this Scripture is fulfilled in your hearing."
>
> —Luke 4:17–21, mev

Yeshua is God incarnate, the Good Shepherd who lays His life down for His sheep, and one of the biggest aspects of His ministry is to heal broken hearts. There are some things that happen to us in life that we could never recuperate from apart from the supernatural healing power of God. Because of Messiah Yeshua, we can have confidence that our hearts can and will heal.

Beloved, if you've been wounded in life, I encourage you to believe Yahweh Rohi will restore your soul. Make this a matter of prayer. If you ask Him daily to restore your soul, you'll find that little by little, day by day, month by month, and year by year, He will put the fractured pieces of your heart together again. You don't have to question whether it is God's will to heal your hurts. Messiah Jesus came to heal the brokenhearted and restore your soul.

The atonement of Jesus makes us whole, for the Bible says, "Surely our griefs He Himself bore, and our sorrows He carried....The chastening for our well-being fell upon Him, and by His scourging we are healed" (Isa. 53:4–5).

Yahweh Rohi Guides Us

David went on to say Yahweh Rohi guides us in the paths of righteousness (v. 3). This means He guides us in His ways, which are the right paths.

If we are putting our trust in the Lord, we can have confidence that when we go astray, He will get us back to the center of His will. He will open doors no one can shut, shut doors no one can open, and bring things into our lives that keep us moving on the right path. I liken what He does to the bumpers many bowling alleys use for kids. When those railings are in place, even if the ball veers, it won't go into the gutter because the bumpers will cause it to stay on the lane. This is what Yahweh Rohi does to guide us in paths of righteousness. Like those bumpers, He keeps us on track even if we veer a little to the left or right. His shepherding keeps us centered and moving forward in Him.

It gives me so much comfort and security to know it's not all up to me to get everything right all the time. *If I am looking to the Father,* I can trust Him to guide me. Of course, that doesn't mean every thought I think and every step I take will be the right one, and it certainly doesn't give any of us a license to sin. It means as I keep my eyes on Yahweh Rohi, He is going to move me in the way I should go.

Yahweh Rohi Protects Us

Verse 4 goes on to say, "Even though I walk through the valley of the shadow of death, I fear no evil, for You are with me." It's important to realize that David didn't write Psalm 23 sitting in a palace basking in the sun as people served him wine. He was in the midst of battle. His enemies were in hot pursuit. Yet in the middle of what was a dangerous situation in the natural, David declared, "I fear no evil, for You are with me."

It's no secret that we live in a dangerous world. The news is filled with reports of global conflict, mass shootings, cyberattacks, natural disasters, moral bankruptcy, chaos, and more. But we don't have to fear because our God is bigger than this world. At least a hundred times in Scripture, Father God tells us not to fear but *to be strong and courageous.* Following are just a few instances:

> Do not fear them, for the LORD your God is the one fighting for you.
>
> —DEUTERONOMY 3:22

Be strong and courageous, do not be afraid or tremble at them, for the LORD your God is the one who goes with you. He will not fail you or forsake you.

—DEUTERONOMY 31:6

Have I not commanded you? Be strong and courageous! Do not tremble or be dismayed, for the LORD your God is with you wherever you go.

—JOSHUA 1:9

Do not fear, for I am with you; do not anxiously look about you, for I am your God. I will strengthen you, surely I will help you, surely I will uphold you with My righteous right hand.

—ISAIAH 41:10

For thus the LORD spoke to me with mighty power and instructed me not to walk in the way of this people, saying, "You are not to say, 'It is a conspiracy!' in regard to all that this people call a conspiracy, and you are not to fear what they fear or be in dread of it. It is the LORD of hosts whom you should regard as holy. And He shall be your fear, and He shall be your dread. Then He shall become a sanctuary."

—ISAIAH 8:11–14

No matter what is happening in the world around us, we don't have to be afraid because the Lord is with us. Messiah Jesus said, "Lo, I am with you always, even to the end of the age" (Matt. 28:20). The Lord never leaves us or forsakes us. Whenever you feel fear trying to take root in your heart, remind yourself of the previous verses and hear Yahweh Rohi declaring over your life, "Do not be afraid, for I am with you."

Yahweh Rohi Gives Us Victory

Yahweh Rohi not only protects us, but He also prepares a table before us in the presence of our enemies (v. 5). In other words, we can be confident God is going to bring justice.

Like many of God's people in Scripture, we often wonder why the wicked prosper. We think, "Why do people who don't care about God seem to succeed while I'm struggling in life? I'm seeking You, Father, and trying to do what's right. Why do I have all these problems?" But the Lord says just hang on because He's going to create a feast before us, and even our enemies are going to see it.

You're going to be rewarded for everything you've done out of your love and obedience to God. When Yeshua returns, many who are last will be first, and many who are first will be last (Matt. 20:16). Your enemies will not triumph over you. When you see Jesus face to face, you're going to feel complete freedom and victory as Yahweh Rohi prepares a feast for you in the presence of your enemies.

Yahweh Rohi Anoints Us and Overtakes Us With Goodness

David went on to write in verse 5, "You have anointed my head with oil." Father God wants to pour out His Spirit on us more and more as we seek Him. We must believe God for this, beloved, and ask Him for more of it. Jesus said, "If you then, being evil, know how to give good gifts to your children, how much more will your heavenly Father give the Holy Spirit to those who ask Him?" (Luke 11:13). The Lord is our Shepherd. He's alive and active in our lives, and

He will pour out such blessing that our cup overflows, just as His Word says (Mal. 3:10; Luke 6:38; 3 John 2).

Then David finishes his psalm saying in verse 6, "Surely goodness and lovingkindness will follow me all the days of my life, and I will dwell in the house of the LORD forever." It's hard not to fear the future, to worry about what will happen to our loved ones, what will happen to us when we get old, whether we will have enough money to retire—the list goes on and on. The devil constantly tries to torment us with fear and oppress us with a spirit of gloom and doom. But you know what I've discovered? It never turns out the way the enemy says. Father God is faithful, and what His Word says is true: *surely goodness and lovingkindness will follow us all the days of our lives.*

We must reject the spirit of gloom and doom. We must reject fear of the future. We don't have to constantly think something bad is going to happen to us or our family members. We don't have to fear tomorrow or growing old. The Lord has declared something totally different over us. He has said surely goodness and lovingkindness will follow us all the days of our lives. Those thoughts of doom, fear, and destruction aren't true. They are lies. They are false evidence appearing real, as the saying goes.

Father God has good plans for you. Goodness and lovingkindness are going to *pursue* you all the days of your life. That's the sense we get from the original Hebrew. The verse isn't indicating that lovingkindness and goodness will follow us from behind. The Hebrew implies that they'll overtake us, that God's goodness and lovingkindness actually chase His children down and overtake them.

The Lord wants us to be happy and confident in Him. Let's

break any agreements we've made in our hearts and minds with spirits of gloom and doom, fear, and destruction. Let's break agreement with those lying thoughts and come into agreement with what Father God says. Let's believe Yahweh Rohi loves us. His plans for our future are good.

Follow the Good Shepherd

Our God wants us to experience Him as Yahweh Rohi, and we do that by following Him. Yeshua said, "My sheep hear My voice, and I know them, and they follow Me; and I give eternal life to them, and they will never perish; and no one will snatch them out of My hand" (John 10:27–28).

Messiah Jesus laid down His life so we could experience the covenant blessing of knowing God as Yahweh Rohi. But if we want to live in that reality, we must not only hear His voice; we must also follow Him in obedience. We don't have to be perfect; we just have to be open and strive to do the best we can. He will do the rest.

CHAPTER 12

YAHWEH TSIDKENU—
THE LORD OUR
RIGHTEOUSNESS

O F ALL THE names Father God has revealed to us, Yahweh Tsidkenu, "the Lord our Righteousness," is one that blesses me the most. God is holy, and we must be righteous to stand before a holy God, but as we saw in chapter 9, we cannot make ourselves holy. So how can we look at ourselves in a mirror and declare ourselves righteous?

I don't know about you, but in the natural I don't feel like I can do that. When I look in the mirror, I don't feel righteous. I may have lost my temper or said something I regret. The Shema from Deuteronomy 6 says, "You shall love the LORD your God with all your heart and with all your soul and with all your might" (v. 5). I question whether I have ever loved God in the fullest possible way. Jesus said, "You shall love the Lord your God with all your heart, and with all your soul, and with all your strength, and with all your *mind*" (Luke 10:27). It's hard to feel that I love God with all my mind when my mind wanders to this or to that.

I can think of many mistakes I've made in the past. But the fact is, we can't make ourselves righteous; it is a gift of God. Yahweh sent Jesus to shed His blood for our sins so we could stand righteous before Him. This was His plan long before Yeshua walked the earth. He spelled it out in the Book of Jeremiah when He revealed Himself as Yahweh Tsidkenu, the Lord our Righteousness.

> "Behold, the days are coming," declares the LORD, "when I will raise up for David a righteous Branch; and He will reign as king and act wisely and do justice and righteousness in the land. In His days Judah will be saved, and Israel will dwell securely; and this is His name by which He will be called, 'The LORD our righteousness [Yahweh Tsidkenu].'"
>
> —JEREMIAH 23:5–6

In this passage we see the Tanakh and the B'rit Hadashah—the Old and New Testaments—fitting together like a hand in a glove. The prophet Jeremiah was given the revelation of Yahweh Tsidkenu at a time when the kingdom of Judah (made up of the tribes of Judah and Benjamin, while the other ten tribes composed what was known as Israel) was grievously refusing to repent of their sins. As a result, Father God allowed them to be attacked by the Babylonian empire and taken into captivity.

Even though Yahweh cut off the Davidic monarchy around 586 BC, just as Jeremiah and Ezekiel prophesied, He promised to raise up for David a righteous Branch, a king who would reign forever with wisdom, justice, and righteousness. This righteous Branch is Yeshua HaMashiach,

Jesus the Messiah. He confers His righteousness to those who put their faith in Him, allowing us to stand righteous before God forever. In other words, the Lord makes us righteous because Messiah Jesus becomes our righteousness.

The Hebrew word *tsidkenu*, meaning "our righteousness," comes from combining the Hebrew words *ṣedeq* (or *tsedek*), which means "straight" or "right,"[1] with the possessive pronoun *nu*, which means "our." It is closely related to the words *ṣadîq*, which means "righteous," and *tzaddik*, which refers to a righteous person.[2] To be righteous is simply to be right, not in the sense of winning an argument but in terms of our standing before God. Yahweh Tsidkenu, the Lord our Righteousness, has made us right with God through the righteous Branch, Messiah Yeshua.

The Great Exchange

No one is righteous in and of himself. Righteousness is a free gift given to us through the blood of Yeshua. Paul said, "He made Him who knew no sin [Jesus] to be sin on our behalf, so that we might become the righteousness of God in Him" (2 Cor. 5:21).

Jesus died in our place, taking our sin in His body and giving us His righteousness in return. This is the great exchange. God's Word declares that the Father "chose us in Him before the foundation of the world, that we would be holy and blameless before Him" (Eph. 1:4). Before the creation of the world, God in His love chose us to be holy and blameless before Him. This is the only way we can become righteous—by being drawn to Yeshua and receiving His righteousness, which He freely bestows on us.

We cannot attain this righteousness through our own

works. The Bible says, "He saved us, not on the basis of deeds which we have done in righteousness, but according to His mercy, by the washing of regeneration and renewing by the Holy Spirit, whom He poured out upon us richly through Jesus Christ our Savior" (Titus 3:5–6). Our sin was transferred into the body of Jesus on the cross. He took our sin in Himself, died in our place, and gave us His righteousness.

No one is righteous apart from God's gift of righteousness. We read in both the Old and New Testaments that there is none righteous, not even one:

> God has looked down from heaven upon the sons of men to see if there is anyone who understands, who seeks after God. Every one of them has turned aside; together they have become corrupt; there is no one who does good, not even one.
>
> —Psalm 53:2–3

> As it is written, "There is none righteous, not even one; there is none who understands, there is none who seeks for God; all have turned aside, together they have become useless; there is none who does good, there is not even one."
>
> —Romans 3:10–12

The word *righteous* is first found in Genesis 7:1: "Then the LORD said to Noah, 'Enter the ark, you and all your household, for you alone I have seen to be righteous [ṣadîq] before Me in this time.'" If not for the grace of God, not even Noah could have been considered righteous. Mankind cannot claim righteousness in and of himself. The prophet Isaiah tells us, "All of us have become like one who is unclean, and all our righteous deeds are like a filthy garment" (Isa. 64:6).

God alone is righteous; He is the absolute standard of righteousness.

Our righteousness comes only from God, so no one can boast of his or her righteousness. The apostle Paul said that if anyone had a right to boast in his flesh, he did. He was born of the tribe of Benjamin, circumcised on the eighth day, and a Pharisee educated under Gamaliel, the leading Jewish sage of his day. Concerning the Law, Paul looked blameless. Yet he said:

> But whatever things were gain to me, those things I have counted as loss for the sake of Christ. More than that, I count all things to be loss in view of the surpassing value of knowing Christ Jesus my Lord, for whom I have suffered the loss of all things, and count them but rubbish so that I may gain Christ, and may be found in Him, not having a righteousness of my own derived from the Law, but that which is through faith in Christ, the righteousness which comes from God on the basis of faith.
>
> —PHILIPPIANS 3:7–9

No one, not even Paul, can boast of his own righteousness. We can only boast in God, who has freely given us His righteousness through Messiah Jesus. Even obeying the Law can't make a person righteous; in fact, Paul said, "By the works of the Law no flesh will be justified in His sight; for through the Law comes the knowledge of sin" (Rom. 3:20). The very purpose of the Law was to make us aware that we are sinners and unable to save ourselves.

The Scriptures tell us that in the gospel, "the righteousness of God is revealed from faith to faith; as it is written, 'But the righteous man shall live by faith'" (Rom. 1:17). Righteousness can only be obtained through our faith in

Messiah Yeshua because He became the ultimate sacrifice for our sin.

Yeshua—the Ultimate Sacrifice

In the Old Testament, the animal sacrifices offered in the Tabernacle were a foreshadowing of Yeshua's ultimate sacrifice for our sin. God had the Tabernacle built so He could dwell among His people and fellowship with them. If an Israelite worshipper desired to meet with God, he had to go to the Tabernacle with a blood sacrifice in the form of an unblemished animal, and the priest would bind it on the altar. The worshipper would then place his hands on the head of the sacrifice and lean his weight into the animal, symbolically transferring his sin into the sacrifice. The animal was then put to death, dying in the worshipper's place.

The worshipper now stood innocent before the Lord because his sin had been transferred into the sacrifice. God accepted the animal sacrifices as an atonement for the sin of His people much the same way a merchant accepts a credit card. Merchants accept credit cards because they know the real payment is coming. Once the credit card runs through the bank, real money will be transferred into the merchant's account. The animal sacrifices were like credit cards; Yeshua's sacrifice is the real payment Yahweh has received.

This system of animal sacrifice was a picture of what Messiah Yeshua would later do for all humanity on the cross. Jesus absorbed our sin into His body and was then put to death in our place. We often speak of the excruciating pain Messiah Yeshua endured when He died on the cross, but I truly believe His physical suffering did not compare to the agony Jesus felt when He absorbed all our sin into His body.

This must have been far harder to endure than the physical pain of dying on the cross.

The Scriptures say that when Yeshua was on the cross, He cried out, "'*Eli, Eli, lama sabachthani*?' that is, 'My God, My God, why have You forsaken Me?'" (Matt. 27:46). *Eli* is a form of *Elohim*, which describes God as the supreme Creator of the universe. When Yeshua was on the cross, He literally cried out to the Master of the universe, "Why have You forsaken Me?"

Jesus said this because He wasn't only experiencing a physical death; He was experiencing the pain of the Father turning His face from Him as He took in His own body the sin of all mankind. At this point Yeshua felt utterly alone, disconnected, and cut off from all life. Jesus literally experienced the second death for us—eternal separation from God.

Because Yeshua, the sinless Son of God, took the sin of all mankind in Himself, we can be made righteous before God by faith in Him. Beloved, our righteousness is not based on how good or bad we've been; it's based on what Yeshua did on the cross. It's as if He's the One standing before God in our place. Those of us who are truly in Messiah Jesus are deemed righteous because Yeshua is the Banner of righteousness over our lives.

I want to stress again that it's impossible for us to make ourselves righteous. God will reward us for the righteous deeds we do in His name, but our good works don't justify us. This is the point Yeshua was making in the parable of the Pharisee and the tax collector.

> And He also told this parable to some people who trusted in themselves that they were righteous, and viewed others with contempt: "Two men went up into the

temple to pray, one a Pharisee and the other a tax collector. The Pharisee stood and was praying this to himself: 'God, I thank You that I am not like other people:
swindlers, unjust, adulterers, or even like this tax collector. I fast twice a week; I pay tithes of all that I get.'

"But the tax collector, standing some distance away,
was even unwilling to lift up his eyes to heaven, but was
beating his breast, saying, 'God, be merciful to me, the
sinner!' I tell you, this man went to his house justified
rather than the other; for everyone who exalts himself will
be humbled, but he who humbles himself will be exalted."

—Luke 18:9–14

In this parable, the Pharisee mistakenly believed he stood
righteous before God based on his own deeds. Yet Jesus said
the Pharisee wasn't the one declared righteous but rather
the tax collector, who humbly repented of his sin. Through
his faith, the tax collector received the free gift of righteousness Yeshua died to give us.

Human righteousness falls short; sinners are justified
before God only when Messiah's righteousness has been
bestowed on them. Those who are in Messiah Jesus can
be confident that they are righteous before God because
Yeshua's righteousness has freely been imparted to them.
When we are in Yeshua, He is our source of righteousness
and the One in whom we should boast.

Isaiah 53 is the strongest prophecy in the Hebrew Bible,
or the Old Testament, that spells out how Yeshua took our
sins and made us righteous in Himself.

All of us like sheep have gone astray, each of us has
turned to his own way; but *the* Lord *has caused the
iniquity of us all to fall on Him.* He was oppressed and
He was afflicted, yet He did not open His mouth; like

a lamb that is led to slaughter, and like a sheep that is silent before its shearers, so He did not open His mouth. By oppression and judgment He was taken away; and as for His generation, who considered that He was cut off out of the land of the living for the transgression of my people, to whom the stroke was due? His grave was assigned with wicked men, yet He was with a rich man in His death, because He had done no violence, nor was there any deceit in His mouth.

But the Lord *was pleased to crush Him, putting Him to grief; if He would render Himself as a guilt offering,* He will see His offspring, He will prolong His days, and the good pleasure of the Lord will prosper in His hand. As a result of the anguish of His soul, He will see it and be satisfied; *by His knowledge the Righteous One, My Servant, will justify the many, as He will bear their iniquities.* Therefore, I will allot Him a portion with the great, and He will divide the booty with the strong; because He poured out Himself to death, and was numbered with the transgressors; yet He Himself bore the sin of many, and interceded for the transgressors.

—Isaiah 53:6–12

We see this entire portion of Scripture beautifully fulfilled in the Gospels. Yeshua was oppressed and afflicted, yet when He stood before Pilate, He kept silent. He was judged and called a blasphemer. He was accused of being the guilty one, and the punishment that should have been taken out on you and me was placed on Him. He had done no violence, nor was there any deceit in His mouth, but Yahweh Tsidkenu was pleased to crush Him, and by knowing this righteous One—the tzaddik—the many become righteous.

Yeshua is the incarnation of Yahweh Tsidkenu; He is the visible image of the invisible God (Col. 1:15). "By His doing

[we] are in Christ Jesus, who became to us wisdom from God, and righteousness and sanctification, and redemption" (1 Cor. 1:30).

Declare Your Righteousness

Through the sin of one man, Adam, all men sinned and were made unjust. But Father God reversed the process, and through the obedience of one man, Messiah Jesus, all who put their faith in Him are made righteous. This is what Paul was speaking of in Romans 5:18–19:

> So then as through one transgression there resulted condemnation to all men, even so through one act of righteousness there resulted justification of life to all men. For as through the one man's disobedience the many were made sinners, even so through the obedience of the One the many will be made righteous.

If you've received Messiah Yeshua through faith, then His righteousness has become yours. This isn't just rhetoric. This is your reality. Some people say, "God could never forgive my sin." They may think they are being humble, but this is actually a perverted form of pride because they're suggesting their sin is greater than God's ability to make them righteous. There is no sin too great for the blood of Yeshua to forgive. Jesus' shed blood, His death, and His resurrection are greater than the power of any sin.

Too many of us are allowing the enemy to continually condemn us. We beat ourselves up over past mistakes and think God is mad at us. Beloved, God is not going to punish our sins twice. Father God allowed Messiah Jesus to be spit on, bruised, beaten, and put to death in our place, and then to experience the second death for us, and He's not going to make us pay the penalty for our sins all over again. He loves us; if He didn't, He wouldn't have sent Jesus, His Son, to die for our sins. At times Father God will correct and discipline His children, but He does this because He loves us and wants to bring us into obedience to His will.

Satan will accuse us day and night to make us think we're unrighteous. He wants us to live in constant condemnation so we'll be emotionally separated from God. When Satan attacks us with shame and condemnation over past sin that we have repented of and given to Jesus, we must stand up against the enemy and reject his lies. Remind him of Paul's words in Romans 8: "Therefore there is now no condemnation for those who are in Christ Jesus. For the law of the Spirit of life in Christ Jesus has set you free from the law of sin and of death" (vv. 1–2).

I encourage you to look at yourself in a mirror and declare, "Yahweh Tsidkenu is my righteousness, and I am righteous in Messiah Jesus." It doesn't matter whether you feel righteous. Your righteousness isn't based on what you think about yourself or what you have or haven't done. Yahweh Tsidkenu is the Lord your righteousness, and you, Baruch HaShem (Bless the Name), have been made righteous in Messiah Jesus!

CHAPTER 13

YAHWEH SHAMMAH— THE LORD IS THERE

IN THE VERY last sentence of the Book of Ezekiel, Father God declares Himself Yahweh Shammah, which means "the Lord is there" or "the Lord is present." "The city shall be 18,000 cubits round about," Ezekiel declares, "and the name of the city from that day shall be, 'The LORD is there [Yahweh Shammah]'" (Ezek. 48:35). As we can see from the context of this verse, Yahweh Shammah is both one of God's Hebrew names and the name of a city. That city is the new Jerusalem described in Revelation chapters 21 and 22.

> Then I saw a new heaven and a new earth; for the first heaven and the first earth passed away, and there is no longer any sea. And I saw the holy city, new Jerusalem, coming down out of heaven from God, made ready as a bride adorned for her husband. And I heard a loud voice from the throne, saying, "Behold, the tabernacle of God is among men, and He will dwell among them, and they shall be His people, and God Himself will be

among them, and He will wipe away every tear from
their eyes; and there will no longer be any death; there
will no longer be any mourning, or crying, or pain; the
first things have passed away."

...And he carried me away in the Spirit to a great and
high mountain, and showed me the holy city, Jerusalem,
coming down out of heaven from God....I saw no temple
in it, for the Lord God the Almighty and the Lamb are
its temple. And the city has no need of the sun or of the
moon to shine on it, for the glory of God has illumined
it, and its lamp is the Lamb.

—Revelation 21:1–4, 10, 22–23

Because Ezekiel speaks of both past and future events, to
fully appreciate what he is telling us when he reveals the
Lord as Yahweh Shammah, we must understand the context
of the Book of Ezekiel.

Written while the people of Israel were in exile in Babylon
as a result of their rebellion against God, Ezekiel describes
God's judgment on them for the sins they committed. Their
sin reached such a height that in one of his visions the
prophet saw God's presence leave the Temple. But the Lord
didn't leave His people without hope. In the last part of the
book Ezekiel paints a picture of the restoration of God's
people in the age to come when the Temple, which was in
ruins, would be rebuilt and God's glory would again dwell
in Jerusalem.

This is a profound prophecy. Although the prophet saw
the horror of God's glory leaving the Temple in Ezekiel 11, he
later saw God's majesty magnificently return and exclaimed,
"The glory of the Lord filled the house" (Ezek. 43:5). In fact,
it is in the last sentence of Ezekiel's book that Yahweh reveals
Himself as Yahweh Shammah in relationship to the new

Jerusalem in the age to come. The insight and revelation we gain here is that this *koinonia* moment of the new Jerusalem happens when heaven and earth collide and the glory of God literally becomes the actual Temple. Yahweh is there.

Although we are not experiencing God in His fullness right now, He is still here. Jesus said, "Lo, I am with you always, even to the end of the age" (Matt. 28:20).

So many of us are fearful about the future. We worry about what our lives will be like when we get old, if our health will begin to fail, or if we'll run out of money. We consider all these negative scenarios the devil tries to put in our minds. But Father God is saying today, "My child, I love you, and I am there in the future. Whatever happens in the days to come, I will be there."

Beloved, the Lord is always present, and He wants us to have confidence. He's not a faraway God we can reach only by shouting to Him; rather, He's closer to us than our own heartbeat. The apostle Paul tells us that the word of faith "is near you, in your mouth and in your heart" (Rom. 10:8). It is not so far away that we can't reach it. Neither is God so far removed that we can't find Him. His Word is in our mouths and in our hearts.

God wants us to know how intimately acquainted with us He is, that He is in every breath we take. He's in every beat of our hearts. God wants us to realize that He's inside us and we belong to Him. In Yeshua, we're in God and God is in us. The Word tells us "in Him we live and move and have our being" (Acts 17:28, MEV). Jesus wants us to know and realize that wherever we go, He is there.

If we think about the future and are afraid, it's because we're envisioning a future without God in it. Sometimes we imagine a circumstance that produces anxiety, but if we really consider the thoughts that are causing us distress, we'll realize that God is not in those thoughts. We don't see Him in those scenarios playing out in our minds. The truth is that wherever you go, God will be there. "He Himself has said, 'I will never desert you, nor will I ever forsake you'" (Heb. 13:5). God will always be in our future. When we experience fear because of a thought about the future, it's because an awareness of God's presence is not in that thought projection. It is not an enlightened thought.

I once heard a story about a girl who for many months had been living in fear of getting fired from her job. She was constantly anxious about it, even losing sleep. After months in this torment, one day she was called into her boss' office, and he fired her. The woman's testimony is that when she actually got fired, she wasn't afraid. Why? Because God was with her when it actually happened.

In our fearful thoughts about the future, we don't sense God. Why? Because God is the God of the present, the God of the now, not the God of vain imaginations that don't actually exist. Yeshua said, "Do not worry about tomorrow; for tomorrow will care for itself. Each day has enough trouble of its own" (Matt. 6:34).

Elsewhere Yeshua said, "I am in the Father and the Father is in Me" (John 14:11). That's how close Messiah Jesus was to the Father when He walked this earth, and that's how close Father God is to us today. He is so close to us, it's beyond words. It's hard to describe something that is nearer to us than our own heartbeat, but that is how close Father God is to us. Scripture says nothing can separate us from the love of God—"neither death, nor life, nor angels, nor principalities, nor things present, nor things to come, nor powers, nor height, nor depth, nor any other created thing" (Rom. 8:38–39). He is with us always, "even to the end of the age" (Matt. 28:20).

Yahweh Shammah—the Glory of the Age to Come

As I wrote in *The Book of Revelation Decoded*,[1] this is what I see Scripture teaching about the end times: when the seventh and last trumpet of God's judgment sounds, the dead who have been redeemed by the Lamb will rise and meet the Lord in the air, along with the believers living during the tribulation. This will mark the long-awaited marriage union between Yeshua and His bride, the church, and will kick off the greatest celebration ever: the marriage supper of the Lamb (Rev. 19:6–9). While believers experience heights of ecstasy and joy, we cannot imagine what those in the world will experience when God's wrath is poured out in its fullness. Once His wrath has been emptied, Jesus will then return to earth.

When He returns, the Lord will save the entire nation of Israel, utterly destroy His enemies, and rid the planet of all wickedness. With His authority now unquestioned, Jesus will sit in the judgment seat and, much to the delight of those who serve Him, reward believers for their deeds on earth. Yet in this same seat He also will judge the sin of the unredeemed and send Satan to the bottomless pit for a thousand years. This will mark the beginning of the millennial reign of Yeshua HaMashiach, who will lead the greatest kingdom the earth has ever known.

And just as every kingdom has a capital where the heart of that nation's government lies, so the Lord will set up the centerpiece of His authority from Jerusalem.

Jerusalem is the world's spiritual summit. Though the city is currently divided, the Lord promised that He will build His house again in Jerusalem. Much like Ezekiel, Zechariah prophesied its rebuilding for the millennial kingdom more than twenty-five hundred years ago:

> Thus says the LORD of Hosts: I have a great jealousy for Jerusalem and Zion....I have returned to Jerusalem with mercy, and My house will be built in it, says the LORD of Hosts, and a measuring line will be stretched over Jerusalem...Yet again My cities will overflow with goodness, and again the LORD will comfort Zion and choose Jerusalem.
>
> —ZECHARIAH 1:14, 16–17, MEV

Indeed the light of the Lord will emanate out of the highest spiritual point, Jerusalem, and flood the world with its truth, righteousness, justice, peace, and love. "Out of Zion, the perfection of beauty, God has shined," the psalmist prophesied in Psalm 50:2 (MEV).

Isaiah described it this way:

> In the last days, the mountain of the LORD's house shall be established on the top of the mountains, and shall be exalted above the hills, and all nations shall flow to it. Many people shall go and say, "Come, and let us go up to the mountain of the LORD, to the house of the God of Jacob, and He will teach us of His ways, and we will walk in His paths." For out of Zion shall go forth the law, and the word of the LORD from Jerusalem.
>
> —ISAIAH 2:2–3, MEV

As the righteous government of the Lord pours out of Jerusalem, yet another prophecy from the Tanakh will become reality: "The earth will be filled with the knowledge of the glory of the LORD, as the waters cover the sea" (Hab. 2:14). This is why we are commanded to "pray for the peace of Jerusalem" (Ps. 122:6). As I said in a previous chapter, there will not really be peace in Jerusalem until the Messiah returns. The only way shalom will rule in Jerusalem is through divine intervention.

The overwhelming character of the new Jerusalem will be Yahweh Shammah—"the Lord is there." It will be "a time of glory, and peace, and joy, and truth, and righteousness," the nineteenth-century preacher Charles Spurgeon said.[2]

Theologian G. Campbell Morgan wrote that the name Yahweh Shammah "tells of complete satisfaction; that of God, and that of man. God is seen at rest among His people, His original purpose realized. Man is seen at rest in God, his true destiny reached." John, from the island of Patmos, in describing the heavenly city, wrote: "Behold, the tabernacle of God is with men, and He shall dwell with them, and they shall be His peoples; and God Himself shall be with them, and be their God."[3]

From the beginning God's longing has been to be one with His people and creation. He has always desired a people who desire Him. In Moses' day the Israelites rejected His offer to come close and be with them; they preferred to keep a safe distance from this awesome, holy God (Exod. 20:19). So God stayed near to them through the Tabernacle (Exod. 25). He later tried to come close to Israel through His prophets, but they too were shunned or ignored.

Although God's plan to be one with His people was partially fulfilled at Yeshua's first coming, most Jewish people rejected Him just as they had in the past. Yet God's longing to be one with all His people will be fulfilled in the last days. All Israel will cry out to Him and recognize Yeshua as the Messiah when He returns. Again, this will usher in the millennial age, when heaven will come to earth. There will be no sorrow, sickness, suffering, or pain. Peace and beauty will exist in every corner of the world. In fact, the physical landscape will be different because nature will be completely restored and no longer permeated with the elements of death or decay. All creation will adhere to the Lord's ruling spirit of shalom, just as Isaiah prophesied:

> The wolf also shall dwell with the lamb, and the leopard shall lie down with the young goat, and the calf and the young lion and the fatling together....The cow and the bear shall graze; their young ones shall lie down together; and the lion shall eat straw like the ox. The nursing child shall play by the hole of the asp, and the weaned child shall put his hand in the viper's den. They shall not hurt or destroy in all My holy mountain, for the earth shall be full of the knowledge of the LORD, as the waters cover the sea.
>
> —ISAIAH 11:6–9, MEV

Creatures that once lived as enemies in violent pursuit or fear of each other will suddenly dwell side by side in complete harmony. All creation will exist in peace with one another because we all will be fully submitted to the Prince of Peace, Jesus Christ. Isaiah continued his vivid description of Yeshua's millennial kingdom at the end of his prophetic book:

> The voice of weeping shall no longer be heard in [the land], nor the voice of crying. There shall no longer be an infant who lives only a few days nor an old man who has not filled out his days....They shall not labor in vain

nor bring forth children for trouble; for they are the
descendants of the blessed of the LORD and their offspring with them....The wolf and the lamb shall feed
together, and the lion shall eat straw like the bull.
—ISAIAH 65:19–20, 23, 25, MEV

If it sounds like the Garden of Eden before mankind fell,
that is because once again it will be. Jesus' second coming
will cleanse the earth of its evil and sin, and His millennial
kingdom will restore it to its perfect original state. Heaven
and earth will be united.

> He made known to us the mystery of His will according
> to His good pleasure, which He purposed in Christ,
> with regard to the fulfillment of the times [that is, the
> end of history, the climax of the ages]—to bring all
> things together in Christ, [both] things in the heavens
> and things on the earth.
> —EPHESIANS 1:9–10, AMP

One of the greatest aspects of the garden in addition to
the perfect creation surrounding Adam and Eve was the
perfect union between them and the Lord. Adam and Eve
shared a pure intimacy with the Lord that allowed them to
walk naked and unashamed before Him.

The millennial kingdom will reintroduce humanity to a
closeness with God so profound and fulfilling that nothing
we have experienced up to this point in life even comes
close to it.

Remember, we were created in the image of Elohim, our
Creator, to have relationship with Him. When Yeshua rap-
tures the church and we are finally united with Him in
the marriage supper of the Lamb, our relationship will be

restored to an intimacy that surpasses even what Adam and Eve had before the fall. We will walk in the fullness of our purpose. We will be married to Yeshua; He will be our husband, and we will be His bride.

This has always been Messiah Yeshua's endgame—to be with us. One day we will physically abide with Him in our new bodies forever. But until then, as we endure the hardships of life on earth, we can have confidence that we're never alone. Yahweh Shammah is always with us. Even when we can't see what is happening, the Lord is already there and moving on our behalf.

PART III

THE HEBREW NAMES OF MESSIAH

CHAPTER 14

YESHUA—MESSIAH'S HEBREW NAME

BEFORE THE MESSIAH was born, an angel told Yosef (Joseph) that Myriam (Mary), his betrothed, would bear a son, "and you shall call His name Jesus, for He will save His people from their sins" (Matt. 1:21). The name translated "Jesus" is *Yeshua* in Hebrew, which means "he will save."[1] This is fitting, for the Scriptures say, "There is no other name under heaven that has been given among men by which we must be saved" (Acts 4:12).

Some people, however, insist Jesus' Hebrew name isn't Yeshua but Yahshua, since Yahshua includes the same "yah" sound found in the name Yahweh. But according to Michael L. Brown, a Messianic Jewish scholar who holds a PhD in ancient Semitic languages spoken during biblical times, there is no support for this whatsoever. In fact, he says there is no such name as Yahshua, only Yeshua, which is simply a shortened form of the name Yehoshua (Joshua in English), much like Dan is a shortened form of Daniel.

Unlike Yahshua, the name Yeshua can be found almost

169

thirty times in the Old Testament, a primary example being Zechariah 3, which refers to a Hebrew high priest who lived after the Babylonian exile. It is interesting that although this high priest's formal name was Yehoshua, he was more frequently referred to as Yeshua as is seen in Ezra 3:2.

As many as ten men in the Hebrew Scriptures were named Yeshua or Yehoshua, indicating it was a common name during that time.[2]

Calling Upon Messiah as Jesus

There are some people who claim it is wrong to refer to Messiah by the name Jesus because they say it was derived from the name of the Greek god Zeus. But Brown says this too is nonsensical and based on linguistic ignorance. The name Jesus is not a corrupt way of rendering the Greek name Zeus; rather, it reflects the Greek way of rendering *Yeshua*.[3]

Two hundred years before the birth of Messiah, scholars translated the Hebrew Scriptures into Greek, creating what is called the Septuagint. When the Hebrew name Yeshua was translated to Greek, it became *Iesous*. Then later when the Greek was translated to Latin, *Iesous* became *Iesus*. And finally, when the Latin was translated to English, *Iesus* became *Jesus*.

The English name Jesus was not derived from the pagan god Zeus; it resulted from the natural progression of translating a name from one language to another: Hebrew to Greek, Greek to Latin, and finally Latin to English.

Going from the Hebrew name Yeshua to the English name Jesus is a very natural transition. It's the same as referring to Yeshua's mother, Myriam, as Mary in English. There's nothing pagan about saying Mary instead of Myriam. One rendering is Hebrew, and the other is English.

Personally, I love Jesus by all His names, no matter the language! When I came to faith in 1978, it was through a vision I received from God in the middle of the night. Jesus appeared on the cross, and a ray of red light beamed from the sky straight down upon His head. At the time, as a Jewish person, I had never heard the Hebrew name Yeshua, but as an American, I knew the person on the cross was Jesus.

God used this vision to show me that Jesus is the way to Him. My early salvation experience was founded in the name Jesus, and I don't believe there's anything wrong with calling our Messiah by that name.

Yeshua—the Only Means of Salvation

Whether He is called Jesus or Yeshua, He is the only way to salvation. The name Yeshua comes from the root word *yāšaʿ*, which means to save, deliver, and rescue,[4] and as I said previously, it is a shortened form of the name Yehoshua, which means "God is salvation."[5] It is vital for us to understand that within Yeshua's very name is the promise of salvation.

We see this in the New Testament where Luke writes:

> Let it be known to all of you and to all the people of Israel, that by the name of Jesus Christ the Nazarene, whom you crucified, whom God raised from the dead— by this name this man stands here before you in good health. He is the stone which was rejected by you, the builders, but which became the chief corner stone. And there is salvation in no one else; for there is no other name under heaven that has been given among men by which we must be saved.
>
> —ACTS 4:10–12

And in the Old Testament, the Scriptures speak of El Yeshuatenu, the God of our salvation, and El Yeshuati, the God of my salvation, who is Yeshua.

Isaiah prophesied that salvation would come through Yeshua:

> Behold, God is my salvation [El Yeshuati], I will trust and not be afraid; for the LORD GOD is my strength and song, and He has become my salvation.
>
> —ISAIAH 12:2

And David sang that Yeshua is the God of our salvation:

> Blessed be the Lord, who daily bears our burden, the God who is our salvation [El Yeshuatenu].
>
> —PSALM 68:19

The name Yeshua is above every other name! At His name, "every knee will bow, of those who are in heaven and on earth and under the earth, and…every tongue will confess that Jesus Christ is Lord, to the glory of God the Father" (Phil. 2:10–11). Some will call Him Jesus, others Yeshua, but all will confess that He is Lord!

The Book of Revelation tells us that one day a great multitude from every tribe, tongue, and nation will gather around the throne of God and worship Messiah Jesus. Each person will be speaking his native language, whether that is Hebrew, Greek, English, or something else. In this beautiful passage of Scripture, it's clear their focus will not be on the language they're speaking but on Yeshua.

> After these things I looked, and behold, a great multitude which no one could count, *from every nation and all tribes and peoples and tongues*, standing before the

throne and before the Lamb, clothed in white robes, and palm branches were in their hands; and they cry out with a loud voice, saying, "Salvation to our God who sits on the throne, and to the Lamb." And all the angels were standing around the throne and around the elders and the four living creatures; and they fell on their faces before the throne and worshiped God, saying, "Amen, blessing and glory and wisdom and thanksgiving and honor and power and might, be to our God forever and ever. Amen."

—Revelation 7:9–12

No matter what language you use, whether you call Him Yeshua or Jesus, He is worthy of our praise and adoration, and when you call on Him in purity and sincerity, your worship will be acceptable and pleasing to Him!

In the next several chapters we will examine other names by which Yeshua is revealed in the Hebrew Scriptures that point us to who He is and what He will do in our lives!

CHAPTER 15

MASHIACH—THE ANOINTED ONE

Y**OU MAY HAVE** heard Jesus referred to as Yeshua HaMashiach. This is the Hebrew way of saying Jesus the Messiah, or Jesus the Anointed One. *Mashiach* means "messiah," or "anointed one," and *ha* simply means "the." So Yeshua HaMashiach means "Jesus the Anointed One. The Greek word for "anointed one" is *Christ*. So to say Jesus Christ is also to say Yeshua is the Anointed One.

Some have thought that Christ is Jesus' last name, but it is not. In the days when Scripture was written, individuals were not referred to by their last name but rather by who they were the son of, or who their father was. Consider, for example, the following passages:

> From the *sons of* Benjamin were Sallu the *son of* Meshullam, the *son of* Hodaviah, the *son of* Hassenuah, and Ibneiah the *son of* Jeroham, and Elah the *son of* Uzzi, the *son of* Michri, and Meshullam the *son of* Shephatiah, the son of Reuel, the *son of* Ibnijah.
>
> —1 CHRONICLES 9:7–8

The record of the genealogy of Jesus the Messiah, the *son of* David, the *son of* Abraham: Abraham was the *father of* Isaac, Isaac the *father of* Jacob, and Jacob the *father of* Judah and his brothers. Judah was the *father of* Perez and Zerah by Tamar, Perez was the *father of* Hezron, and Hezron the *father of* Ram.

—Matthew 1:1–3

The word *mashiach* is used many times in Scripture, including when Daniel prophesies the timing of the Messiah's first coming to earth.

So you are to know and discern that from the issuing of a decree to restore and rebuild Jerusalem until Messiah [*mashiach*] the Prince there will be seven weeks and sixty-two weeks; it will be built again, with plaza and moat, even in times of distress. Then after the sixty-two weeks the Messiah [*mashiach*] will be cut off and have nothing, and the people of the prince who is to come will destroy the city and the sanctuary. And its end will come with a flood; even to the end there will be war; desolations are determined.

—Daniel 9:25–26

Many historians believe the weeks in Daniel's prophecy were actually periods of seven years, and each year was made up of 360 days. So Daniel was prophesying that there would be sixty-nine seven-year periods, or roughly 483 years, between the command to rebuild the Temple and the coming of the Messiah. The clock for the "seven weeks and sixty-two weeks" began around 445 BC when Artaxerxes, the king of Persia, gave Nehemiah the order to rebuild the Temple (Neh. 2:1–8). In his book *The Coming Prince*, theologian Sir Robert Anderson calculates that, adjusting for leap years, 483 years (or 173,880 days) ends in AD 32, when Messiah Jesus was in the midst of His earthly ministry. Some scholars even believe the timing aligns to the day when Yeshua made His triumphal entry into Jerusalem.[1]

Daniel's Messianic prophecy, like so many others, was fulfilled in Yeshua.[2] He is the "one like a Son of Man" whom Daniel saw in a vision being presented before the Ancient of Days—"and to Him was given dominion, glory and a kingdom, that all the peoples, nations and men of every language might serve Him. His dominion is an everlasting dominion which will not pass away; and His kingdom is one which will not be destroyed" (Dan. 7:13–14).

Yeshua is the Messiah, the Anointed One Daniel spoke of.

Set Apart

In the Hebrew Scriptures the concept of anointing someone carries with it the idea of consecrating them and setting them apart to serve God in a particular office or function. In ancient times priests and kings were ceremonially anointed to signify they had been appointed to that position and God's power was upon them. For instance, when God established the Levitical priesthood, He instructed Moses to "anoint [Aaron and his sons] and ordain them and consecrate them, that they may serve Me as priests" (Exod. 28:41). Priests were chosen to draw near to the divine presence, offer sacrifices on Israel's behalf, and bless God's people. Today, you and I likewise are chosen to be in relationship with our God, and to pray for others and bless them on His behalf.

Oftentimes we see God using oil as a symbol of this consecration and Spirit empowerment. When David was anointed king of Israel, the prophet Samuel poured oil on him, which symbolized David's appointment to that office and the Spirit of God on his life. The Bible says after "Samuel took the horn of oil and anointed him in the midst of his brothers...the Spirit of the LORD came mightily upon David from that day forward" (1 Sam. 16:13).

Jesus too was anointed before He began His earthly ministry. When Yeshua was baptized in the Jordan River, the Bible says "heaven was opened, and the Holy Spirit descended upon Him in bodily form like a dove, and a voice came out of heaven, 'You are My beloved Son, in You I am well-pleased'" (Luke 3:21–22). When the Holy Spirit descended on Yeshua, Father God was consecrating and commissioning Him to fulfill His plan to save humanity from the penalty of our sins.

The Anointing of the Anointed One

Yeshua wasn't anointed with the special mixture of oil the Levitical priests used in the Hebrew Scriptures. He instead received the Ruach HaKodesh, the One the anointing oil represents. But because the ancient priesthood was a shadow of Messiah Yeshua's function as the great High Priest (Heb. 9–10), understanding the type of oil used to anoint the Levitical priests will help us better grasp the anointing that is on Yeshua HaMashiach, the Anointed One.

The oil used to anoint the priests is described in detail in Exodus 30:

> Moreover, the LORD spoke to Moses, saying, "Take also for yourself the finest of spices: of flowing myrrh five hundred shekels, and of fragrant cinnamon half as much, two hundred and fifty, and of fragrant cane two hundred and fifty, and of cassia five hundred, according

to the shekel of the sanctuary, and of olive oil a hin. You shall make of these a holy anointing oil, a perfume mixture, the work of a perfumer; it shall be a holy anointing oil. With it you shall anoint the tent of meeting and the ark of the testimony, and the table and all its utensils, and the lampstand and its utensils, and the altar of incense, and the altar of burnt offering and all its utensils, and the laver and its stand.

"You shall also consecrate them, that they may be most holy; whatever touches them shall be holy. You shall anoint Aaron and his sons, and consecrate them, that they may minister as priests to Me. You shall speak to the sons of Israel, saying, 'This shall be a holy anointing oil to Me throughout your generations. It shall not be poured on anyone's body, nor shall you make any like it in the same proportions; it is holy, and it shall be holy to you.'"

—Exodus 30:22–32

This passage reveals some important truths about the anointing that is on Messiah Yeshua.

He is anointed with beauty

Myrrh, cinnamon, cane, and cassia are some of the finest, most fragrant spices on earth, and all these beautifully scented ingredients were mixed with olive oil to produce a perfume-like oil used to anoint God's priests. I don't believe it is coincidental that the anointing oil was so fragrant. I believe its beautiful scent is prophetically symbolic of the beauty of Yeshua.

Many of us don't recognize the beauty of God. We see His masculine qualities, such as His great power and might, but we fail to see His beauty. God is beautiful, beloved, and His creation reflects His splendor. We see His beauty in the majestic trees, the radiant sun, and the magnificent mountains and rivers. We see it in the vibrant, colorful flowers.

I love being in nature, and when I look at certain flowers, I sometimes think the yellows couldn't be any more yellow; the oranges, reds, and purples couldn't be any richer. Even with all the sophistication of modern technology, we can't create color as beautiful as what exists naturally in these flowers. And they're all just a reflection of how beautiful Yeshua is.

The Creator of the universe describes Himself as "the rose of Sharon, the lily of the valleys" (Song of Sol. 2:1). He is altogether lovely (Song of Sol. 5:16, KJV)!

The beauty of God is so incredible that David said encountering it was the one thing he wanted above all else.

> One thing I have asked from the LORD, that I shall seek: that I may dwell in the house of the LORD all the days of my life, to behold the beauty of the LORD and to meditate in His temple.
>
> —PSALM 27:4

David wanted to know God for who He is, in the fullness of His beauty and majesty.

Yeshua is not just all-powerful and all-knowing; He is also beautiful. Because of the anointing on Yeshua, we can exchange our ashes for His beauty and experience abundant life in Him (Isa. 61:3, MEV; John 10:10).

He is anointed with joy

If you look at some Christians, you might think following Jesus is a boring chore. Their faces are joyless, their expressions lifeless. But Yeshua has been anointed with joy, and He came to give us "the oil of joy for mourning" (Isa. 61:3, MEV).

The psalmist said of Yeshua:

> Your throne, O God, is forever and ever; a scepter of uprightness is the scepter of Your kingdom. You have loved righteousness and hated wickedness; *therefore God, Your God, has anointed You with the oil of joy above Your fellows.*
>
> —PSALM 45:6–7

The writer of Hebrews says:

> But of the Son He says, "Your throne, O God, is forever and ever, and the righteous scepter is the scepter of His kingdom. You have loved righteousness and hated lawlessness; therefore God, Your God, has anointed You with the oil of gladness above Your companions."
>
> —HEBREWS 1:8–9

Father God has anointed Yeshua with the oil of gladness. We serve a happy God, and we can be full of joy through the anointing that is on Messiah Jesus!

He is anointed with power

Yeshua is not only beautiful and full of joy; He has been anointed with power to heal every disease and cast demons out of those oppressed by the evil one. Peter spoke of this in a sermon to the Gentiles in the Book of Acts:

> You know of Jesus of Nazareth, how God anointed Him with the Holy Spirit and with power, and how He went about doing good and healing all who were oppressed by the devil, for God was with Him.
>
> —ACTS 10:38

Regardless of where you are or where you've been, Yeshua has the power to destroy the works of Satan in your life. As you completely submit yourself to Him and yield to His Spirit, Jesus will literally crush Satan under your feet (Rom. 16:20).

The Ruach HaKodesh has anointed Messiah Jesus to bring good news to the afflicted, heal the brokenhearted, free the captives, comfort those who mourn, and turn ashes into beauty. We see this powerful declaration in Isaiah 61:

> The Spirit of the Lord GOD is upon me because the LORD has *anointed* me to preach good news to the poor; He has sent me to heal the broken-hearted, to proclaim liberty to the captives, and the opening of the prison to those who are bound; to proclaim the acceptable year of the LORD and the day of vengeance of our God; to comfort all who mourn, to preserve those who mourn in Zion, to give to them beauty for ashes, the oil of joy for mourning, the garment of praise for the spirit of heaviness, that they might be called trees of righteousness, the planting of the LORD, that He might be glorified.
>
> —ISAIAH 61:1–3, MEV

Jesus read from this very passage in the Tanakh when He began His public ministry and said, "Today this Scripture has been fulfilled in your hearing" (Luke 4:21), drawing a straight line from the words of Isaiah to the anointing on His life.

Much like the Old Testament priests were anointed with a special fragrant oil, so too Yeshua has been anointed with the Holy Spirit and imbued with the fragrant oil of beauty, joy, and power. As you abide in Him, the Anointed One, the same anointing that is on Him will be imparted to you. You will receive His beauty, joy, and power to crush Satan under your feet.

CHAPTER 16

TSEMACH—THE BRANCH

O NE OF THE revelatory descriptions of the Messiah revealed to us in the Hebrew Bible is that He is the *Tsemach*, the Branch.

> Now listen, Joshua the high priest, you and your friends who are sitting in front of you—indeed they are men who are a symbol, for behold, I am going to bring in *My servant the Branch*.
>
> —ZECHARIAH 3:8

> "Behold, the days are coming," declares the LORD, "when I will raise up for David a righteous *Branch*; and He will reign as king and act wisely and do justice and righteousness in the land."
>
> —JEREMIAH 23:5

A branch is a secondary shoot arising from a main source or something that extends from a main body.[1] Yeshua is the shoot arising from the main source, Father God. He is an extension of the Father, and He receives life from Him. This is what Yeshua was referring to when He said, "I am in the

Father, and the Father is in Me" (John 14:10). The apostle John also pointed this out when he wrote that Jesus is "the only begotten God who is in the bosom of the Father" (John 1:18).

Yeshua is the Tsemach, the Branch who extends to us from Father God. We see this again in Isaiah, which speaks of a Branch that will come from the root of Jesse, the father of David, and walk in the power of the Ruach HaKodesh.

> Then a shoot will spring from the stem of Jesse, and a branch from his roots will bear fruit. The Spirit of the LORD will rest on Him, the spirit of wisdom and understanding, the spirit of counsel and strength, the spirit of knowledge and the fear of the LORD.
>
> —Isaiah 11:1–2

There is no question this Messianic prophecy is referring to Jesus because Yeshua Himself said, "I am the root and the descendant of David, the bright morning star" (Rev. 22:16). Jesus is the Branch, and He instructed us to abide in Him so we will become branches that shoot forth from Him and bear fruit.

In one of His last messages before He endured the agony of the cross, Jesus told His disciples:

> Abide in Me, and I in you. As the branch cannot bear fruit of itself unless it abides in the vine, so neither can you unless you abide in Me. I am the vine, you are the branches; he who abides in Me and I in him, he bears much fruit, for apart from Me you can do nothing.
>
> —John 15:4–5

Isaiah prophesied that within the Tsemach will be "the spirit of wisdom and understanding, the spirit of counsel and strength, the spirit of knowledge and the fear of the

LORD" (11:2). This is the fruit we too will bear by abiding in Yeshua.

The Spirit of Wisdom

When we abide in Messiah Yeshua, the Branch, we'll begin to exhibit a spirit of wisdom. Even if we know a specific truth, it will have little effect if we lack the wisdom to apply it. For example, we may know the truth that we are to be witnesses for the Lord, but we need wisdom to know when and how to speak to be successful and fulfill that call.

Wisdom is the ability to apply God's truth appropriately in any given situation. It helps us know when someone needs encouragement and when he needs to be confronted about turning from his sin. Wisdom gives us balance so we don't take one biblical truth to such an extreme that we veer into heresy. We need wisdom to know how to raise our children and grandchildren. We need wisdom to know how to navigate relationships.

The Bible says, "Wisdom is the principal thing; therefore get wisdom" (Prov. 4:7, KJV). If we are to be effective followers of Yeshua, we must have a spirit of wisdom. As we abide in Yeshua, we will become more like Him, including growing in wisdom. And the good news is, all we have to do is keep seeking and asking, and we will receive more and more of it, for the Bible says, "But if any of you lacks wisdom, let him ask of God, who gives to all generously and without reproach, and it will be given to him" (Jas. 1:5).

The Spirit of Understanding

Another fruit of abiding in Yeshua is the spirit of understanding. This is the ability to comprehend something, to have insight and perception. Understanding helps us see more than just what is evident on the surface.

For example, we may view a prostitute as being the worst of all sinners, but when God looks at that prostitute, He has understanding. He knows she grew up without a father, and her mother was a drug addict and a prostitute herself. God still recognizes prostitution as a sin, but He has understanding as to why the woman ended up in that lifestyle.

Beloved, if we're going to truly reflect the heart of Yeshua, we need depth of sight in the Spirit in order to have understanding to perceive how life and reality work. Wisdom is like a primordial knowing. Understanding helps us to intellectually apprehend why things are so.

The Spirit of Counsel

As we abide in Yeshua, we'll begin to walk in the spirit of counsel. In the natural, a counselor analyzes a situation and then gives helpful advice to guide a person to make the right decision or necessary changes in his life. The Holy Spirit does this for us in real time. He is our great Counselor, the trustworthy guide for our lives.

Father God said, "I will instruct you and teach you in the way which you should go; I will counsel you with My eye upon you" (Ps. 32:8). This is what the Ruach HaKodesh was sent to do.

Yeshua, the Branch, said, "But the Counselor, the Holy Spirit, whom the Father will send in My name, will teach you everything and remind you of all that I told you" (John 14:26, MEV). When we lean on the Holy Spirit as our Counselor, He will give us the direction we need for our lives and the wisdom to counsel others.

The Spirit of Strength

Another fruit we'll bear as we abide in the Branch is the spirit of strength. This enables us to stand in the power of Yeshua and battle our enemy, Satan. No one can avoid this warfare. We must boldly resist the devil if we're going to be victorious.

Seven times in the first three chapters of Revelation, Yeshua tells us of the rewards that will be granted to those who overcome:

> To him who overcomes, I will grant to eat of the tree of life which is in the Paradise of God.
>
> —Revelation 2:7

> He who overcomes will not be hurt by the second death.
>
> —Revelation 2:11

> To him who overcomes, to him I will give some of the hidden manna, and I will give him a white stone, and a new name written on the stone which no one knows but he who receives it.
>
> —Revelation 2:17

> He who overcomes, and he who keeps My deeds until the end, to him I will give authority over the nations; and he shall rule them with a rod of iron, as the vessels of the potter are broken to pieces, as I also have received authority from My Father; and I will give him the morning star.
>
> —Revelation 2:26–28

> He who overcomes will thus be clothed in white garments; and I will not erase his name from the book of life, and I will confess his name before My Father and before His angels.
>
> —Revelation 3:5

> He who overcomes, I will make him a pillar in the
> temple of My God, and he will not go out from it any-
> more; and I will write on him the name of My God,
> and the name of the city of My God, the new Jerusalem,
> which comes down out of heaven from My God, and
> My new name.
>
> —Revelation 3:12

> He who overcomes, I will grant to him to sit down with
> Me on My throne, as I also overcame and sat down with
> My Father on His throne.
>
> —Revelation 3:21

Those verses remind us that we need to be willing to fight, beloved. This life won't always be easy; in fact, Yeshua said in the world we will have tribulation (John 16:33). We will need to go to war with the enemy if we're going to overcome and live in victory.

I wrestled back in high school, and when I finished a match, I could hardly breathe. Wrestling was excruciatingly painful because I had to fight with all my strength to win. This is the posture we must have as followers of Yeshua.

The Bible says, "For our struggle is not against flesh and blood, but against the rulers, against the powers, against the world forces of this darkness, against the spiritual forces of wickedness in the heavenly places" (Eph. 6:12). There is a spiritual battle constantly going on all around us. Every day when we wake up, the enemy is right there trying to get us to doubt, trying to distract us, trying to make us fearful and get us to rely on ourselves.

We need to learn to "be strong in the Lord and in the strength of His might" (Eph. 6:10). We must resist doubt, discouragement, and the pressures of the world and fight for truth. We need to stand up in Messiah Yeshua, and we can't do that without His strength.

I've cast demons out of people's lives, but if the person doesn't continue to fight and resist the devil, those demons will return, and he or she will be worse off than before (Matt. 12:44–45). King Saul was tormented by a demon, and whenever it attacked him, he would call David to play the harp. While David was playing his instrument, the demon would leave Saul, but as soon as David left, it would return (1 Sam. 16:14–23). That's the way it is with the enemy. We can't rely on someone else to fight for us and solve our problems. We must find strength in the Lord and learn to fight for ourselves. There's no other way to victory.

Ephesians 6 gives us a blueprint for how to battle the enemy.

> Therefore, take up the full armor of God, so that you will be able to resist in the evil day, and having done everything, to stand firm. Stand firm therefore, having girded your loins with truth, and having put on the breastplate of righteousness, and having shod your feet with the preparation of the gospel of peace; in addition to all, taking up the shield of faith with which you will be able to extinguish all the flaming arrows of the evil one. And take the helmet of salvation, and the sword of the Spirit, which is the word of God.
>
> —Ephesians 6:13–17

To stand firm against our adversary we have to be fully clothed in the armor of God. We need to gird our loins with truth, believing God instead of Satan. We must put on the breastplate of righteousness, which means we stand confidently in the righteousness Yeshua imparted to us when we chose to put our faith in Him. We also must walk in the peace of God that passes all understanding by getting in touch with Yeshua, who lives inside us, and clinging to the shield of our faith so we'll be able to withstand the attacks of the enemy. We also need to cover our heads with the helmet of salvation by reminding ourselves not just that we're saved but also who we are as children of God. And finally, we must hold tightly to the sword of the Spirit, the Word of God, which equips us to counter Satan's lies with the truth.

As we clothe ourselves daily in God's armor, we will be equipped in the spirit of strength to prevail against the enemy and live in victory.

The Spirit of Knowledge

When we abide in the Branch, we are also equipped with the spirit of knowledge. Knowledge is information we have acquired through experience, revelation, and study that is divine. The types of knowledge the Lord gives are diverse. For example, in 1 Corinthians 12:8 Paul speaks about a spiritual gift called "the word of knowledge," which is the ability to know facts about a situation or person that are not attained by the natural but are given by a revelation of the Spirit. For instance, in a public gathering the minister may say, "There's somebody here who has gum disease, and you are scheduled for surgery on Thursday, but God is healing you right now." If you ever watched Pat Robertson on *The 700 Club*, you may have seen or heard him do something like this.

The type of knowledge the Spirit gives often depends on your calling. For example, the Scriptures tell us the Lord blessed Bezalel and Oholiab with the knowledge of craftsmanship to help build the Tabernacle and its furnishings.

> Then Moses said to the sons of Israel, "See, the LORD has called by name Bezalel the son of Uri, the son of Hur, of the tribe of Judah. And *He has filled him with the Spirit of God, in wisdom, in understanding and in knowledge* and in all craftsmanship; to make designs for working in gold and in silver and in bronze, and in the cutting of stones for settings and in the carving of wood, so as to perform in every inventive work. He also has put in his heart to teach, both he and Oholiab, the son of Ahisamach, of the tribe of Dan. He has filled them with skill to perform every work of an engraver and of a designer and of an embroiderer, in blue and in purple and in scarlet material, and in fine linen, and of a weaver, as performers of every work and makers of designs."
>
> —EXODUS 35:30–35

Through the spirit of knowledge, God gives us the information we need to accomplish His will.

The Spirit of the Fear of the Lord

Finally, as we abide in the Branch, we'll walk in the spirit of the fear of the Lord. People often avoid things that make them uncomfortable. This is why many believers don't want to read the Book of Revelation—because it deals with the frightening reality of hell. But in truth, Revelation was given to be a blessing to us. John said, "Blessed is he who reads and those who hear the words of the prophecy, and heed the things which are written in it; for the time is near" (Rev. 1:3). Even though it contains sobering truths, Revelation was written to bless us.

Fear is not always bad; it can alert us to danger and keep us out of harm's way. The same thing happens spiritually. The fear of God's judgment can keep us from sinning. If you think about it, one reason children behave is that they fear being punished. They have a healthy fear of being disciplined that helps them stay on the right path. The same thing can happen with us as followers of Jesus.

The Lord wants us to have a healthy fear of Him because "the fear of the LORD is the beginning of wisdom" (Prov. 9:10). Like any loving parent, Father God doesn't want us to be afraid of Him, but He wants us to respect Him as the Master of the universe, the Adon Olam. He wants us to recognize His sovereignty and preeminence. The psalmist said, "Let all the earth fear the LORD; let all the inhabitants of the world stand in awe of Him. For He spoke, and it was done; He commanded, and it stood fast" (Ps. 33:8–9).

Isaiah 8:12–14 says: "You are not to say, 'It is a conspiracy!' in regard to all that this people call a conspiracy, and you are not to fear what they fear or be in dread of it. It is the LORD of hosts whom you should regard as holy. And He shall be your fear, and He shall be your dread. Then He shall become a sanctuary."

We should be praying for the fear of the Lord. The Bible says, "Behold, the eye of the LORD is on those who fear Him, on those who hope for His lovingkindness, to deliver their soul from death and to keep them alive in famine" (Ps. 33:18–19). I want the eye of the Lord to look in my direction. I want to be preserved in dry seasons. Don't you? A healthy fear of God will lead us to honor Him, deepen our faith, and keep us walking in obedience.

Beloved, let's abide in Yeshua Tsemach, the Branch. He came bearing the fruit of wisdom, understanding, counsel, strength, knowledge, and the fear of the Lord. As we rest in Him, cling to Him, and depend on Him, the same fruit will begin to spring forth from our lives.

CHAPTER 17

SHILOH—THE TRANQUIL ONE WHO HAS SECURED DOMINION

NOTHER NAME FOR Messiah in the Hebrew Bible is *Shiloh* (pronounced shee-low). *Shiloh* means "the tranquil One who has secured dominion." The name is found in a prophecy Jacob (later renamed Israel) issued to his twelve sons—from whom we get the twelve tribes of Israel—shortly before his death, and it is a code name for Messiah. The great Jewish commentator Rashi declares that Shiloh is Mashiach. This is why we say Yeshua HaMashiach.

In his prophecy, which is recorded in the Book of Bereshit, or Genesis, Jacob said this to his son Judah:

> The scepter shall not depart from Judah, nor the ruler's staff from between his feet, until Shiloh comes, and to him shall be the obedience of the peoples.
>
> —GENESIS 49:10

Genesis 49:10 is one of many prophecies in the Torah that speak of the Messiah coming through the lineage of Judah. Matthew very intentionally demonstrates in his Gospel that Yeshua fulfilled this Messianic prophecy, showing that He not only descended from Abraham, Isaac, and Jacob, as the Hebrew Scriptures foretold (Gen. 17:19; 21:12; Num. 24:17), but that He came specifically through the tribe of Judah.

> The record of the genealogy of Jesus the Messiah, the son of David, the son of Abraham: Abraham was the father of Isaac, Isaac the father of Jacob, and Jacob the father of Judah and his brothers. Judah was the father of Perez and Zerah by Tamar, Perez was the father of Hezron, and Hezron the father of Ram....So all the generations from Abraham to David are fourteen generations; from David to the deportation to Babylon, fourteen generations; and from the deportation to Babylon to the Messiah, fourteen generations.
>
> —Matthew 1:1–3, 17

From the time of Abraham to the birth of Messiah Yeshua, God kept His covenantal, prophetic line in place. In fact, in John's apocalyptic finale, the Book of Revelation, Yeshua is specifically identified as the One whom Genesis 49:10 foresaw: "And one of the elders said to me, 'Stop weeping; behold, the Lion that is from the tribe of Judah, the Root of David, has overcome so as to open the book and its seven seals'" (Rev. 5:5). Shiloh, the tranquil One from the tribe of Judah who has secured dominion, is the One who holds the scepter, or the ruling rod.

Shiloh Will Bring Peace

The Bible tells us in Psalm 122 to pray for the peace of Jerusalem, and so we should. But the reality is there will not be peace until Shiloh, the tranquil One who has secured dominion, returns. There will be constant turmoil and fighting in Jerusalem until Shiloh returns to earth, takes His seat on the throne of David, and reigns from Jerusalem.

At that time there will be incredible peace on earth because Shiloh will secure dominion and the obedience of the people. He will reign in authority with His ruling rod. The Creator will finally take His place over His creation and secure that which belongs to Him. Sin will not be tolerated, nor will it go unpunished. Shiloh, who has secured dominion, will keep everything in perfect harmony.

Isaiah prophesies of this time when the Messiah reigns and there will be such peace that even the animals will dwell together in tranquility and a child will be safe playing next to a den of cobras.

> And the wolf will dwell with the lamb, and the leopard will lie down with the young goat, and the calf and the young lion and the fatling together; and a little boy will lead them. Also the cow and the bear will graze, their young will lie down together, and the lion will eat straw like the ox. The nursing child will play by the hole of the cobra, and the weaned child will put his hand on the viper's den. They will not hurt or destroy in all My holy mountain, for the earth will be full of the knowledge of the Lord as the waters cover the sea.
>
> —Isaiah 11:6–9

When Shiloh reigns, "the nations will resort to the root of Jesse, who will stand as a signal for the peoples; and His resting place will be glorious" (Isa. 11:10).

Shiloh Is Sovereign

Right now, life on earth is anything but glorious. Every day it seems we hear of another unthinkable atrocity—innocent bystanders are being gunned down in mass shootings, and as hard as it is to face it, children are being kidnapped and sold into sex slavery. The world is so dark that some people wonder whether God really is sovereign. They can believe He is sovereign in heaven, but they question whether we can truly have confidence that God is reigning in our lives when He doesn't appear to be exercising His sovereignty here on the earth.

Beloved, the fact that evil seems to hold sway over the world doesn't mean God is not sovereign. Paul said, "For the mystery of lawlessness is already at work; only he who now restrains will do so until he is taken out of the way" (2 Thess. 2:7). The Holy Spirit has been restraining the enemy and the chaos he wants to unleash in the world. But as we get closer to Yeshua's return, the Holy Spirit will stop exerting the same amount of His authority and government in the world. This will create the environment for the Antichrist to arise, which the Scriptures teach must happen before Jesus returns (2 Thess. 2:3).

As the Holy Spirit begins to draw back, evil is going to rise. That is what we're dealing with right now. We feel it in the culture and in politics. We see it in the brokenness of relationships. Satan is the god of this world, and he is currently exerting his power and influence on the earth

(2 Cor. 4:4). But Yeshua is the Adon Olam, the Master of the universe. He is the One who said, "All authority has been given to Me in heaven and on earth" (Matt. 28:18). Satan will wreak havoc on the earth, but only for a while. God is in control of all things, and in the end Yeshua will reign in victory and Satan will be "cast into the lake of fire and brimstone" where he "will be tormented day and night forever and ever" (Rev. 20:10, mev).

Until then, we must cling to the tranquil One who has secured dominion and trust Him to be sovereign in our lives. As we seek the Lord, draw near to Him, and yield every area of our lives to Him, He will fill us with supernatural peace and security. Yeshua taught us to pray: "Our Father who is in heaven, hallowed be Your name. Your kingdom come. *Your will be done*, on earth as it is in heaven" (Matt. 6:9–10). As we call upon Father God in humility, drawing near to Him and asking Him to be sovereign in our lives, He will respond to that call and reign in our lives and circumstances.

The Lord assures us in Psalm 91 that if we make Him our habitation—if we make Him our resting place—He will protect us. When I am battling fear, this psalm brings real comfort to my heart. Consider with me the first several verses, quoted here from the Amplified Bible:

> He who dwells in the shelter of the Most High will remain secure and rest in the shadow of the Almighty [whose power no enemy can withstand]. I will say of the LORD, "He is my refuge and my fortress, my God, in whom I trust [with great confidence, and on whom I rely]!" For He will save you from the trap of the fowler, and from the deadly pestilence. He will cover you and completely protect you with His pinions, and under His

wings you will find refuge; His faithfulness is a shield
and a wall.

—Psalm 91:1–4, amp

If we cling to the Lord, He is going to cover us, so if we
want His complete protection, we must abide in Him and
depend on Him. We need to be like Moses, who told the
Lord, "If Your presence does not go with us, do not lead us
up from here" (Exod. 33:15). Moses wouldn't move without
God's presence, and we need to be the same way. We should
be afraid to go forward in life if we're not trusting in and
clinging to Shiloh.

To those who make the Lord their refuge, the psalmist
says:

> You will not be afraid of the terror by night, or of the
> arrow that flies by day; of the pestilence that stalks in
> darkness, or of the destruction that lays waste at noon.
> A thousand may fall at your side and ten thousand at
> your right hand, but it shall not approach you....No evil
> will befall you, nor will any plague come near your tent.
>
> —Psalm 91:5–7, 10

Beloved, if we don't want anything to touch our lives that
doesn't first pass through the sovereign hand of God, we
must cling to Him. We must trust Messiah Yeshua to be
Shiloh in our lives—to be our refuge and give us peace in
the midst of the chaos raging all around. As we draw near
to Him, Shiloh will reign over every circumstance we face
and make us victorious in Him.

PART IV

OUR RESPONSE
TO WHO GOD IS

CHAPTER 18

ADONAI—OUR LORD AND MASTER

THE HEBREW NAMES of God covered so far in this book have revealed to us the many ways God has promised to bless and meet the needs of His people. But there is one name that shifts the focus from what God promises to do for us to our responsibility to Him, and that is *Adonai*, which means "Lord" or "Master." When we relate to God as Adonai, the emphasis is on our need to submit ourselves to the Creator. Knowing God as Yahweh Yireh, the Lord our Provider, or Yahweh Shalom, the Lord our Peace, requires us to trust Him to provide for us or give us peace. The burden is on Him to meet our need. But when we call on God as Adonai, the responsibility shifts to us and our need to respond to Him in loving surrender and obedience.

Adonai is found more than four hundred times in the Hebrew Bible in reference to God. A form of Adonai—*adon*—is found about three hundred times, and in several of these cases, *adon* refers to the relationship between a servant and his master. So when we call on God as Adonai, it means we look to Him not only as the One who can bless us but also as our Master. In the new covenant, we are called "servants of Christ" (1 Cor. 4:1). To know God as Adonai is to understand that He is the rightful owner of our lives and our responsibility is to do His will.

Moses understood this. When he called on God as Adonai, Moses took the posture of a servant:

> Then Moses said to the LORD [Yahweh], "Please, Lord [Adonai], I have never been eloquent, neither recently nor in time past, nor since You have spoken to Your *servant*; for I am slow of speech and slow of tongue."
> —EXODUS 4:10

Even though Moses felt unqualified to lead the Israelites out of slavery in Egypt, he understood that he was responsible to submit to what Adonai told him to do. Moses pleaded with the Lord to not make him speak, but in the end he was obedient to the call God had given him. Just as it was with Moses, when we honor God as Adonai, we recognize that we belong to Him and have an obligation to submit to and obey Him.

Whom Do You Serve?

In today's Christian culture many believers love experiencing God's presence, but they aren't willing to truly submit to Him as Adonai. They love how they feel as they're worshipping God, but as soon as they leave the church building, they do whatever they want, and Adonai is pushed to the side. They think of God as a means to get what they want instead of making Him their Master and Lord. It's as if they think He exists to serve them when in reality the opposite is true.

Paul said, "You are not your own...for you have been bought with a price" (1 Cor. 6:19–20). We don't belong to ourselves. Yeshua, the visible manifestation of the invisible Adonai, purchased us for Himself, not "with perishable things like silver or gold...but with precious blood, as of a lamb unblemished and spotless, the blood of Christ" (1 Pet. 1:18–19). We were bought with the shed blood of Yeshua and freed from the power of sin and death. And now, as Jude says, Yeshua is "our only Master and Lord" (Jude 4).

The Maker of the universe wants us to relate to Him as Adonai. He wants to bring us to a place of submission because in that place of surrender and obedience He releases His peace and blessing into our lives.

Contrary to the way the gospel is often taught, there is more to following Yeshua than saying the sinner's prayer. We must surrender our lives to Him. Jesus said, "Not everyone who says to Me, 'Lord, Lord,' will enter the kingdom of heaven, but he who does the will of My Father who is in heaven will enter" (Matt. 7:21). Elsewhere Yeshua said, "If anyone serves Me, he must follow Me" (John 12:26). There are Christians who think they are free to do whatever they please and refuse to be submissive and obedient to God. But Yeshua said, "If you love Me, you will keep My commandments" (John 14:15), meaning our obedience to Him actually reveals our love for Him. If Messiah Yeshua is truly our Adonai, we will respond to Him in obedience.

In a parable in Matthew's Gospel, Yeshua compared those who hear the Word of God and *obey* it to a wise man who built his house on the rock. When the wind and the rain beat against his house, it stood firm because it was built on a strong foundation. But those who do not obey the Word are like a man who built his house on the sand. "The rain fell, and the floods came, and the winds blew and slammed against that house; and it fell—and great was its fall" (Matt. 7:27). When life is chaotic and things seem to be falling apart, those who worship God as Adonai and do what He says will remain steadfast.

Beloved, you and I must understand that we are God's servants, and we honor Him with our surrender and obedience. Father God declared through the prophet Malachi:

> "A son honors his father, and a servant his master [adon]. Then if I am a father, where is My honor? And if I am a master [adon], where is My respect?" says the LORD of hosts to you, O priests who despise My name.
>
> —MALACHI 1:6

The Lord is asking the same questions of us today. Is God truly our Adonai, our Lord and Master? Are we His servants? Do we show Him honor and respect by being submissive and obedient to Him? Do we love Him and desire to bless Him? Has His call on our lives broken down our self-will, or are we unwilling to sacrifice our own pleasure? Are we being faithful to serve the Lord with our talents and all our other resources? Yeshua said, "If anyone wishes to come after Me, he must deny himself, and take up his cross and follow Me. For whoever wishes to save his life will lose it; but whoever loses his life for My sake will find it" (Matt. 16:24–25). We have to go all in—only then will we experience the joy of knowing Him as our Adonai.

Sadly, some believers don't even realize they haven't made

Him their Adonai because many of the invitations to follow Yeshua we hear today are incomplete. People are told that if they want to go to heaven, all they need to do is receive Yeshua into their heart. That's true, but we also need to understand what that means. To receive Yeshua into our heart means we give up our own rights, lay down our agendas, and make Him Lord. Of course, this requires the grace of God.

The Bible says, "If you confess with your mouth Jesus as Lord, and believe in your heart that God raised Him from the dead, you will be saved" (Rom. 10:9). It also tells us every knee will bow and every tongue will confess that Yeshua is Lord (Phil. 2:10–11). At some point, whether in this life or in eternity, everyone will acknowledge that Jesus is Lord. But understand that Yeshua didn't come to earth simply to get people to confess that *He is Lord*. Yeshua didn't call us to simply say a sinner's prayer; He called us to take up our cross and obey Him and make Him Adonai, the Lord of our lives.

If you've never truly surrendered your life to Yeshua, now is the time. (See "Prayer to Make Jesus Your Lord" at the end of this book.)

The apostle Paul gave up everything to follow Messiah Jesus, but he said he counted all his accomplishments and accolades as loss in comparison with knowing Yeshua as his Lord:

> If anyone else has a mind to put confidence in the flesh, I far more: circumcised the eighth day, of the nation of Israel, of the tribe of Benjamin, a Hebrew of Hebrews; as to the Law, a Pharisee; as to zeal, a persecutor of the church; as to the righteousness which is in the Law, found blameless. But whatever things were gain to me, those things I have counted as loss for the sake of Christ.

> More than that, I count all things to be loss in view of
> the surpassing value of knowing Christ Jesus my Lord,
> for whom I have suffered the loss of all things, and
> count them but rubbish so that I may gain Christ.
>
> —Philippians 3:4–8

Messiah Yeshua's disciples gave up all they had to follow Him. Peter said to Jesus, "Behold, we have left everything and followed You" (Matt. 19:27).

When a rich young man came to Messiah asking what he must do to obtain eternal life, Jesus told him, "If you wish to be complete, go and sell your possessions and give to the poor, and you will have treasure in heaven; and come, follow Me." The passage goes on to say, "When the young man heard this statement, he went away grieving; for he was one who owned much property" (Matt. 19:21–22).

Yeshua wasn't saying eternal life could be bought or that good works can save us. He was showing the young man that he would have to release his life and rights in order to fully follow Adonai. Sadly, this rich man seemed unwilling to part with his wealth. Yeshua commented on this episode by saying:

> Truly I say to you, it is hard for a rich man to enter the
> kingdom of heaven. Again I say to you, it is easier for a
> camel to go through the eye of a needle, than for a rich
> man to enter the kingdom of God.
>
> —Matthew 19:23–24

Notice the disciples' response to Yeshua's words:

> When the disciples heard this, they were very aston-
> ished and said, "Then who can be saved?" And looking

at them Jesus said to them, "With people this is impossible, but with God all things are possible."

—MATTHEW 19:25–26

Yeshua said no one can serve God and earthly wealth, "for either he will hate the one and love the other, or he will be devoted to one and despise the other" (Matt. 6:24). He wasn't telling us money is bad; He was saying we cannot love or trust anyone or anything more than Him.

Beloved, we need to put everything else aside and make Jesus our Lord. Messiah said, "The kingdom of heaven is like a merchant seeking fine pearls, and upon finding one pearl of great value, he went and sold all that he had and bought it" (Matt. 13:45–46). I remember once hearing the president of the Bible school I attended say when he was getting out of bed in the morning, the first thing he did was commit himself to God—his mouth, hands, feet, heart—because he wanted to be a servant of Adonai. He began each day by putting God first. What a great example to follow—to commit our entire selves to Adonai each morning before our feet ever touch the ground.

I'm so thankful I can talk with God and bring all my needs to Him. But I also recognize that I have a responsibility to bow my knee to Yeshua and make Him the Lord of my life.

The Cost of Following Adonai

Let us not be deluded into thinking our lives will be devoid of all conflict when we choose to follow Jesus. The opposite is often true. Yeshua is the Prince of Peace, but following Him will cost us something.

The Messiah told us His mission was not to bring peace on earth:

> I did not come to bring peace, but a sword. For I came to set a man against his father, and a daughter against her mother, and a daughter-in-law against her mother-in-law; and a man's enemies will be the members of his household. He who loves father or mother more than Me is not worthy of Me; and he who loves son or daughter more than Me is not worthy of Me. And he who does not take his cross and follow after Me is not worthy of Me. He who has found his life will lose it, and he who has lost his life for My sake will find it.
>
> —MATTHEW 10:34–39

Following Yeshua may create conflict and strained relationships with friends and family. We may have to endure persecution and, in these end times, possibly even lose our lives. But as Paul said, these things pale in comparison to the excellence of knowing Jesus as Lord.

Back in 1978 when I came to faith, following Yeshua cost me everything in terms of my relationships. As a Jewish person, I lost all my friends, and my family thought I was crazy. My parents even probated me to a psychiatric ward for two months and hired the most famous deprogrammer in the country to kidnap and deprogram me so I'd stop believing in Yeshua.

I don't say that to elicit sympathy; I consider it a blessing to suffer with Jesus. But just as it cost me something to follow Him, it will cost you, beloved. Yeshua told His disciples they shouldn't be surprised if the world hates them:

> If the world hates you, keep in mind that it hated me
> first. If you belonged to the world, it would love you as
> its own. As it is, you do not belong to the world, but I
> have chosen you out of the world. That is why the world
> hates you. Remember what I told you: "A servant is not
> greater than his master." If they persecuted me, they will
> persecute you also.
>
> —John 15:18–20, niv

A servant is not greater than his master; if Jesus was persecuted, we can expect to be persecuted too. In fact, we
should be wary if no one ever disagrees with anything
we say. It could be a sign that we're not taking a stand for
Yeshua, that we're not really making Him Lord. If we're following Adonai, we're going to be different. Some will be
attracted to us; some will be repelled. Our lives will reflect
the fruit of knowing Yeshua as Lord, and that is going to
cost us some relationships.

But I tell you from experience, when you're willing to sacrifice to be His, when you're willing to be rejected, laughed
at, and even hated for Him, it fills you with a joy that truly is
beyond comprehension, especially for those who don't know
Jesus. I remember someone once calling me a happy moron.
The person saw the joy of the Lord on my countenance, and
he just couldn't understand it. This person was Jewish, and
he thought it was ridiculous that I could have such joy in the
face of his accusations and scorn. But what he saw was the
joy of the Lord that came from paying the price.

Consider Yeshua's words from the famous Sermon on the
Mount:

> Blessed are those who have been persecuted for the sake
> of righteousness, for theirs is the kingdom of heaven.

Blessed are you when people insult you and persecute you, and falsely say all kinds of evil against you because of Me. Rejoice and be glad, for your reward in heaven is great; for in the same way they persecuted the prophets who were before you.

—Matthew 5:10–12

Beloved, we must be willing to pay the price to follow Yeshua. If we're not, we have to ask ourselves if we've sincerely made Him our Adonai. When we're willing to sacrifice ourselves, be rejected, and suffer for Him, then Yeshua truly is our Adonai.

He will reward us for the sacrifices we make for Him. He will strengthen us in our faith, affirm our identity in Him, and give us the incredible joy and peace that come from knowing nothing can separate us from His love—"neither either death, nor life, nor angels, nor principalities, nor things present, nor things to come, nor powers, nor height, nor depth, nor any other created thing, will be able to separate us from the love of God, which is in Christ Jesus our Lord" (Rom. 8:38–39).

There is a price to pay to make Messiah our Adonai, but great will be our reward.

CONCLUSION

As the Lord led the children of Israel out of Egypt through the wilderness to the Promised Land, He kept making known new dimensions of Himself by giving them a new revelation of His name in response to every need that arose. With each new covenant name revealed to His people came a new understanding of a need they could trust Him to meet. The same is true for us. When we come to know God through the revelation of His names, we can have complete confidence that He will abundantly provide for us just as He did for the people of Israel.

Through these pages we've seen how complete a salvation we have in Him. It's clear that from the very beginning, Father God wanted us to know Him. In the Book of Genesis, He made Himself known to Abraham, Isaac, and Jacob as *Elohim*—the Creator; *El Elyon*—God Most High; and *El Shaddai*—God Almighty.

In Exodus, He made His relationship with mankind even more personal when He introduced Himself to Moses by His personal name, *Yahweh*.

As we study the Torah and the Prophets, we learn who Yahweh wants to be to us by the way He connected His personal, covenant name, *Yahweh*, to all that He does. For example, He revealed Himself as *Yahweh Yireh*, the Lord who Provides, letting us know through this name that He is always going to be there to meet our needs, whether they are physical, emotional, relational, or spiritual. He doesn't promise to give us everything we want, but we can count on Him to sustain us and supply all our needs. He's done this in my life, and He will do the same for every one of His children.

One of my favorite covenant names of God that was first revealed to humanity through the Israelites is *Yahweh Ropheka*, the Lord our Healer. Whatever needs to be healed— whether it's your heart, mind, body, or soul—God is the healer. He can even supernaturally sustain us as we age. I don't understand all there is to know about the Lord. Like many others, I've often wondered why one person is healed immediately, another is healed over time, and still another doesn't experience healing until heaven. I don't have all the answers, but I do know this: we can't let what we don't understand keep us from trusting what we do know is true, which is that God has revealed Himself as Yahweh Ropheka, and "by [Messiah's] stripes we are healed" (Isa. 53:5, NKJV).

The Lord is also *Yahweh Nissi*, our Banner of victory, and through Him we can overcome. We should walk through life with our heads held high because the Bible says God has "raised us up with Him, and seated us with Him in the heavenly places in Christ Jesus" (Eph. 2:6). Elsewhere we're told that "we overwhelmingly conquer through Him who loved us" (Rom. 8:37). Yeshua defeated death, hell, and the grave, and the banner of His victory is over your life and mine. As we lay hold of that truth, we'll see His victory released in our lives more and more as we ascend in the power of the Spirit.

The Lord is not only our victory Banner; He is also *Yahweh M'Kaddesh*, the Lord our Sanctifier. As we cooperate with God, we are supernaturally being changed to look more like Jesus. In a year or two from now, when we look back at our lives, we should see that we're different because the Lord has been sanctifying us and conforming us to the image of His Son, Yeshua (Rom. 8:29).

The Lord wants to fill us with His peace. He is *Yahweh Shalom*, the Lord our Peace, and as we seek Him, God will bring peace and strength into our lives.

He will lead us in paths of righteousness as *Yahweh Rohi*, the Lord our Shepherd, and His goodness and lovingkindness will literally pursue and overtake us all the days of our lives.

Through the Messianic prophecy in the Book of Jeremiah we also saw that Father God is *Yahweh Tsidkenu*, the Lord our Righteousness. We can't be holy in ourselves, but we are righteous in Messiah Jesus. When Yeshua shed His blood on the cross, He took our sin upon Himself and gave us His righteousness instead. So now when we stand before the Father, He sees us as holy and clean because when He looks at us, He sees the righteousness of His Son, Jesus. "By His doing [we] are in Christ Jesus, who became to us wisdom from God, and righteousness and sanctification, and redemption" (1 Cor. 1:30).

Finally, we don't want to ever forget that our God revealed Himself as *Yahweh Shammah*, the Lord Is There, letting us know that no matter what happens in the future, He will always be with us. The Lord promised to never leave us nor forsake us (Heb. 13:5), so wherever we go, we can count on Yahweh Shammah to be there too.

All the covenant promises God made to us through His names are fulfilled in Jesus. His Hebrew name is *Yeshua*, which means to save and rescue. He is the *Mashiach*, the One who is anointed with beauty, joy, and power to destroy the works of the enemy. Yeshua is the *Tsemach*, the Branch, the secondary shoot that extends from the main source, the Father, and causes us to bear much fruit as we abide in Him. And He is *Shiloh*, the tranquil One who reigns; Yeshua is sovereign, and we can trust Him to secure dominion in our lives.

But in order to experience the fullness of who God is, we must make Him our *Adonai*, our Lord and Master. In other words, God is in partnership with us, and we must respond to Him with submission and obedience. We need to not only confess our faith in Yeshua but also recognize that He is the rightful owner of our lives and our responsibility is to surrender to His will.

As we close this book, I want to encourage you to trust that God is who He says He is and will do what He says He will do. Both the Old and New Testaments tell us the Lord does not change but is the same yesterday, today, and forever (Mal. 3:6; Heb. 13:8). As we put our faith in Him, we can expect Him to do and be for us all that He promised through His sacred names.

"For our heart rejoices in Him, because we trust *in His holy name*" (Ps. 33:21).

PRAYER TO MAKE
JESUS YOUR LORD

GOD'S WORD IS full of promises that confirm His love for you and His desire to give you His abundant life. He wants to give you shalom—complete wholeness in your spirit, soul, mind, and body—through a personal relationship with Messiah Jesus.

God loves you, no matter who you are or what you've done in your past. He loves you so much that He gave His only begotten Son for you. The Bible tells us that "whoever believes in Him shall not perish, but have eternal life" (John 3:16). Jesus laid down His life and rose again so we could spend eternity with Him in heaven and experience His fullness here on earth.

Scripture tells us, "If you confess with your mouth Jesus as Lord, and believe in your heart that God raised Him from the dead, you will be saved" (Rom. 10:9). If you've never made a decision to follow Yeshua and would like to receive Him into your life, say the following prayer from your heart.

217

Messiah Jesus, I believe You are the Son of God and that You died for my sins. I also believe You were raised from the dead and now sit at the right hand of the Father praying for me. I ask You to forgive me of my sins and change my heart so I can be Your child and live with You eternally. Help me to walk with You so that I can know You as my Savior and Lord. Jesus, I choose to follow You and ask that You fill me with the power of the Holy Spirit. I declare that right now I am a child of God. I am free from sin and full of the righteousness of God. I am saved in Your name, Yeshua. Amen.

If you prayed this prayer to receive Jesus Christ as your Savior for the first time, I rejoice with you and invite you to contact us at DiscoveringTheJewishJesus.com. We look forward to hearing from you.

If you enjoyed this book and believe other people would benefit from reading it, please leave a review on Amazon.

NOTES

Introduction

1. "What Does Genesis 27:36 Mean?" BibleRef, accessed June 23, 2023, https://www.bibleref.com/Genesis/27/Genesis-27-36.html.

Chapter 3

1. Blue Letter Bible, s.v. "*šaḏ*," accessed June 23, 2023, https://www.blueletterbible.org/lexicon/h7699/kjv/wlc/0-1/.

Chapter 7

1. "Most Americans Believe in Supernatural Healing," Barna Group Inc., September 29, 2016, https://www.barna.com/research/americans-believe-supernatural-healing/.
2. Rabbi K. A. Schneider, *Experiencing the Supernatural* (Grand Rapids, MI: Chosen, 2017), chapter 10.
3. Blue Letter Bible, s.v. "*ya'ăqōḇ*," accessed June 23, 2023, https://www.blueletterbible.org/lexicon/h3290/kjv/wlc/0-1/.

Chapter 9

1. Blue Letter Bible, s.v. "*qāḏôš*," accessed June 23, 2023, https://www.blueletterbible.org/lexicon/h6918/kjv/wlc/0-1/.

Chapter 11

1. Leland Ryken, *Dictionary of Biblical Imagery* (Downers Grove, IL: InterVarsity Press, 1998), 782.

Chapter 12

1. Blue Letter Bible, s.v. "*ṣeḏeq*," accessed June 23, 2023, https://www.blueletterbible.org/lexicon/h6664/kjv/wlc/0-1/.
2. Blue Letter Bible, s.v. "*ṣadîq*," accessed June 23, 2023, https://www.blueletterbible.org/lexicon/h6662/kjv/wlc/0-1/; *Merriam-Webster*, s.v. "tzaddik," accessed June 23, 2023, https://www.merriam-webster.com/dictionary/tzaddik.

Chapter 13

1. Portions of this chapter were adapted from Rabbi K. A. Schneider, *The Book of Revelation Decoded* (Lake Mary, FL: Charisma House, 2017).

2. Charles Spurgeon, "Jehovah-Shammah: A Glorious Name for the New Year," The Spurgeon Center, accessed June 23, 2023, https://www.spurgeon.org/resource-library/sermons/jehovah-shammah-a-glorious-name-for-the-new-year-2/#flipbook/.

3. G. Campbell Morgan, *Searchlights From the Word* (Eugene, OR: Wipf & Stock, 2010), 305.

Chapter 14

1. Blue Letter Bible, s.v. "*yēšûaʿ*," accessed June 23, 2023, https://www.blueletterbible.org/lexicon/h3442/kjv/wlc/0-1/.

2. Michael L. Brown, "Is the Name 'Jesus' Really Related to the Name 'Zeus'?," ASKDrBrown, June 18, 2013, https://askdrbrown.org/article/is-the-name-jesus-really-related-to-the-name-zeus.

3. Brown, "Is the Name 'Jesus' Really Related to the Name 'Zeus'?"

4. Blue Letter Bible, s.v. "*yāšaʿ*," accessed June 23, 2023, https://www.blueletterbible.org/lexicon/h3467/kjv/wlc/0-1/.

5. Blue Letter Bible, s.v. "*yᵊhôšûaʿ*," accessed June 23, 2023, https://www.blueletterbible.org/lexicon/h3091/kjv/wlc/0-1/.

Chapter 15

1. David Guzik, "Daniel 9—the Seventy Weeks of Daniel," Enduring Word, accessed June 23, 2023, https://enduringword.com/bible-commentary/daniel-9/.

2. If you want to learn more about the Messianic prophecies fulfilled in Yeshua, I explore this subject at length in my book *Messianic Prophecy Revealed*.

Chapter 16

1. *Merriam-Webster*, s.v. "branch," accessed June 23, 2023, https://www.merriam-webster.com/dictionary/branch.

DISCOVERING THE JEWISH JESUS

CONNECT WITH RABBI SCHNEIDER

www.DiscoveringTheJewishJesus.com

/Discovering the Jewish Jesus with Rabbi Schneider

facebook.com/rabbischneider

@RabbiSchneider

Roku—Discovering the Jewish Jesus

Apple TV—Discovering the Jewish Jesus

Amazon App—Discovering the Jewish Jesus

Podcast—Discovering the Jewish Jesus

Search for Rabbi Schneider and Discovering the Jewish Jesus on your favorite platform.

For a complete list of Rabbi Schneider's television and radio broadcasts, visit www.DiscoveringTheJewishJesus.com.

223